TALES FROM THE TOP
How CEOs Act and React

by
Simon Ramo

With an
Introduction
by
James Ellis
Dean, USC Marshall School of Business

TALES FROM THE TOP: HOW CEOS ACT AND REACT
by Simon Ramo
is published by
FIGUEROA PRESS
Suite 401E
840 Childs Way
Los Angeles, CA 90089
Phone: (213) 743-4808
Fax: (213) 743-4804
www.figueroapress.com

Figueroa Press is a division of the USC University Bookstore

Cover, text and layout design by USC GraphicDesign

Produced by Crestec Los Angeles, Inc.

Printed in the United States of America

Library of Congress Cataloguing-in-Publication Data
Simon Ramo
TALES FROM THE TOP: HOW CEOS ACT AND REACT
ISBN-13: 978-1-932800-88-3
ISBN-10: 1-932800-88-3
Library of Congress Control Number: 2011934521

Table Of Contents

Preface

When invited some years ago to lecture on business management at the California Institute of Technology and at the University of Southern California, I probed many management books in preparation. They proved helpful, but not in the human dimension of management, the art of dealing with people. Here the texts offered mainly trite advice: "communicate clearly — listen rather than pontificate — motivate others — give praise when due — be considerate but firm." Traveling the book route seemed unlikely to end in arrival at a superior understanding of how executives act or should act.

My bright young auditors aspired to become chief executive officers one day. I thought they should get a feel for the vast array of personal factors — integrity, judgment, ambition, competitiveness, friendliness, determination, ethics, avarice, fear, prejudice, sense of humor, jealousy, immaturity, ageing, egotism — that intertwine and influence profoundly the performance of leaders in management. Appreciating early the relevance, power, and variety of these human traits surely is as vital to success for CEOs as is learning about maximizing return on investment, financing optimally, or marketing aggressively.

To lecture effectively on the natures of managers, I could see, would not be easy. But I chanced upon an approach that made the human factor of business leadership fascinating to the class members. I opened every lecture with a short story. The plots and characters of the fables (some inspired by the adventures of real-life executives) were chosen to enable my listeners, all endowed with copious imagination, to partake vicariously of the circumstances and experiences depicted. Using this approach both the broad scope and much useful detail of the life forces of CEOs could be pictured. Of course, the agitations, excitements, mysteries, and satisfactions involved in directing people are inherently engrossing. The joining and clashing of personalities and the head-on and side-effects when human beings engage in catering to their separate agendas are fascinating of themselves, or should be, to anyone with management ambitions.

Telling good stories — it appeared from the students' eager attention and their comments and questions after they heard the tales — can teach about people better than can the offering of generalities. Of course, the Bible and Shakespeare's plays made this quite clear a long time ago.

The fables that follow had their birth in those oral offerings. I hope that in written form they will prove as interesting and useful to readers as the class members seemed to find them.

Simon Ramo

Introduction

by James Ellis,
Dean, Marshall School of Business
University of Southern California

The moment I chanced upon the short stories that Simon
Ramo had composed for some lectures he was delivering
on management, I knew they would provide the means I
had been seeking for some time to improve the teaching of
the human relations dimension of business management. I
refer here not to the duties of the typical company's human
relations officer, one who deals with workers' unions
problems and with employees' compensation, benefits,
and retirement policies. Such matters are usually rather
adequately presented at business schools. Not usually so
well taught is the human dimension of leadership, how
managers act or should act and react as they deal with other
executives and with their own staffs.

What kind of personalities and character qualities make
for success? How do those in top management handle
"people problems?" What mistakes are most likely to be
made by those in leadership positions as they go about
their duties when it comes to relating to others, those
organizationally above or below them or at their level?

As a dean of a business school I was well aware
that professors in those schools often tell stories in their
classrooms. They recall incidents in their actual experiences
that they deem worth describing to the students so as to

help educate them about important "human relating" fundamentals. This storytelling doubtless is effective as a teaching tool and appreciated by the students. But it was new and attractive to me to make use of fictitious tales that are actually designed especially to emphasize and illuminate those fundamentals. By careful choice and synthesis of plots, characters, issues, and situations, these fictitious stories can be convincingly real life based. They can be constructed so as to present extremely pertinent and useful basics for a new business school course. I felt this so strongly that as Dean of the USC Marshall School of Business I decided to introduce them into the course that I teach.

The class met once a week for two hours for ten weeks, a one semester course. A single tale was assigned to be read and contemplated each week. Each story was accompanied by two lists I prepared. One was of the specific issues raised by that story. The other was of questions the students were asked to ponder and be prepared to discuss in class. I have offered this course now for two years and plan to continue, because it has been clearly a success.

Chapter 1: Philosophy Squared

"I know you're here, Dr. Del Mar, to talk about becoming a director of the Wooley Instruments Corporation. But first let me say how glad I am to have the chance at last to meet with you. You've been president of York College now for, what is it, six or seven months? I attended one trustees meeting where you spoke — you performed brilliantly — but we had no opportunity then to really get acquainted. I've been invited to some social affairs in your honor but darned if each time a business trip or some schedule conflict didn't preclude my attending."

"Well, I hope and expect to be here in York many, many years, Mr. Freeman. So I guess we'll manage to live with a little delay in our getting to know each other well. I'd like nothing better than to become a good friend of yours. I am aware, of course, Mr. Freeman, that you are recognized as York's leading attorney."

"And I am aware that you have taken the town by storm, Stan. I'm going to call you Stan and you must call me Sid. You are not only the youngest president the college has ever had, you're also this area's new social lion. Please forgive my applying such a gauche title to a scholar-statesman. I was born here. I've lived here in York almost all my life. So I'm authoritative when I tell you that we've never had a personality talked about the way you are. All the ladies — they've been competing like mad to get you, to entertain you and your wife in their homes. If I weren't a widower, I'm sure my late wife would have snagged you for a dinner party before now. No wonder Arthur Wooley wants you on the board of his company."

"I feel flattered that he's invited me to join his board."

"Of course, as chairman of the board of trustees of York College, Arthur was also the head of the search committee that found you, Stan. So he naturally feels a special pride in having attracted you to York College. He says you're proving to be even sharper than he thought. Moreover, Arthur tells me, you're an absolutely charismatic personality. So I'm on my guard."

"Ah — I know you're jesting, Mr. Freeman — I mean, Sid. I simply have a few questions — elementary questions to you, I'm sure."

"To a lawyer, elementary questions are the hardest to handle. So now I'm even more on my guard."

"You see, Sid, I've never been on the board of a business corporation, still less of a billion dollar one. As dean of the undergraduate school at Theodore Mann University, I worked closely with its president, Alfred Langer. He was on five corporation boards, and I saw some things that worried me."

"Five Boards? How could Theodore Mann's trustees have allowed that? If he is a good director of five companies, how does he find time to run that university? But, forgive me — I interrupted you."

"It was not just the time those corporate boards required of him, Sid, but the legal depositions he kept getting forced into. They made Langer very uncomfortable. I came to know through his experience what a great risk a director of a publicly held corporation takes on. For instance, the directors can expect to be sued — if not by unhappy shareholders then by disgruntled employees or customers or even the government."

"Well, Stan — we're living in a very litigious society. Corporations, especially large ones, are often sued. You're right about that. Wooley Instruments at the present time has a dozen or so litigation actions against it in progress — not at all unusual for a company its size. But that really shouldn't worry you as a director. A little of your time will be lost if you're called to testify as to something happening with the corporation. But most actions don't go that far. Should you even have to appear for a deposition, you'll never be in any danger. An accidental misstatement or inaccuracy in your testimony isn't going to cause you to be tried for perjury. If you have good attorneys — and Wooley's company has good ones — namely, Freeman, Irving, and Nettleton, if you'll forgive a plug — we see to all that. We protect you. In fact, almost all the time we get the directors excused from having to appear at requested depositions."

"Could we discuss some possible conflicts of interest. Sid? They're really ethics problems, I think, more than legal ones."

"Ethics? You're going to ask a lawyer about questions of ethics? Now, Stan, you've really got me nervous."

"I doubt that, Sid. You must realize, Sid, that not only have I never been on any corporation's board, I've never been close to either the business world or the legal fraternity. I first was a young professor of philosophy, then I was a young university dean, and now I'm a young college president. It happened fast. It didn't enable me to enjoy a lot of experience in dealing with the world outside of academe. So I'm a tyro, a real novice, an innocent, when it comes to both business corporations and the law."

"You're a professional philosopher, aren't you? So you could be expected to have trouble with the nasty real world, despite you're being possessed of remarkable inherent intellectual talents that have gotten you where you are in so short a time."

"I'm a Ph.D., Sid, a doctor of philosophy - in the field of philosophy. That means I'm philosophy <u>squared</u>, or a philosophical <u>square</u>, as my wife likes to tell me."

"Well, ethics and philosophy are surely intertwined, we can say, can't we, Stan? That helps make both ethics and philosophy interesting. Now, let's see, Stan. What are you telling me? Are you worried that if you go on the Wooley board you'll violate some ethical standards you have set for yourself?"

"Well, Sid, consider this: As president of the college I'm beholden to — that is to say, I report to — the college's board of trustees. They hired me. They can fire me. Arthur Wooley is chairman of that board of trustees. He symbolizes that position of responsibility and authority over me. He's my boss, in other words. That's over-simplified, I realize, but in a substantial way it's true."

"Yes, Stan, it's true, to a partial but significant degree."

"Now, at Wooley Instruments, there is a board of directors. It is elected by the shareholders."

"Presumably it is, that is correct — technically — but actually, practically speaking, that's not entirely the way it is. But go ahead, Stan."

"Well — legally the board is responsible for the company, isn't it, Sid? It is given its responsibility and authority by the owners of the corporation, the shareholders. The directors have elected a chairman, Arthur Wooley. The board appointed him chief executive officer and assigned him considerable power. The board can dismiss him if they don't like his performance, just as the board of trustees of York College can oust me."

"Yes. True, in theory. What's the problem?"

"Arthur Wooley reports to the Wooley board. If I join it that means I will have a responsibility to judge him. I will have influence, even if only a little, on whether he holds his job. At the same time he can determine whether I hold mine. Isn't there some conflict there?"

"Not a real one, no. A theoretical one."

"Well, suppose, Sid, that I observe his work as CEO of Wooley Instruments and I find he comes up short. I should say so to the other board members; I should suggest we should dismiss him and get a new CEO, if that's the way I honestly feel. I'm told he owns around ten percent of the stock, but it's a publicly listed corporation with lots of shareholders to whom I have a responsibility to represent them. It's my legal obligation, as a director, to speak up. But am I going to do that when I know that he's a judge of my performance as president of the college? He helps set my salary. Let's say Arthur finds me inadequate for president of the college, but in turn hesitates because I have a vote in assessing him. Is it ethical, for…"

"For a college president to be on the board of a corporation whose chief executive simultaneously is on the board of the college? It happens very commonly, Stan."

"But is it right?"

"It's an issue that comes up often. Mr. A, president of B corporation, is on the board of C corporation whose president, Mr. D, is on the board of B corporation. Such cross membership is very common. The SEC, the Security and Exchange Commission, and the FTC, the Federal Trade Commission -- neither gets bothered about it unless the two corporations are competitive.

"Let me be frank, Stan. You're being extremely, overly, theoretical. You're not familiar with the way things actually work in the corporate world. Now, for instance, I'm the attorney for York College, I'm also the chief attorney for Wooley Instruments Corporation, I'm a trustee of the college, I'm Alan Wooley's personal attorney as well…"

"And you're also on the board of Wooley Instruments. That's why I am particularly interested, Sid, in your opinion on potential conflicts."

"Potential conflicts, Stan. You've hit on the key word, potential. First of all I know well each player involved in these interrelationships. I know all the people and I know the two organizations, the college and the company. Potential conflicts of interest are present, I grant you. However, the mere presence of potential conflicts violates no law. Since the ethics of all the individuals involved in this case are high —."

"I know they are, Sid."

"Well, basically, Stan, that's why the probability that real conflicts of interest will arise is trivial. For example — let's say you do indeed turn out to be the wrong man for president of York College. Do you really think Arthur is going to protect you for fear you'll otherwise retaliate by going against him at Wooley where you're a director? Arthur's position with his board is secure and he knows it. If you were to suggest to Wooley's board that Wooley Instruments needs a new CEO, what would happen? I'll tell you what, Stan. The others on the board would ask you to resign as a board member. If you refused, you would find yourself no longer on the slate of board members to be reelected at the next shareholder's meeting and they'd be rid of you then."

"I see. I understand, Sid. Yes. Let me ask you then a different question that might appear personal to you, Sid, but isn't. As you said, you are the attorney for both the corporation and the college. Now I happen to have noted that Wooley Instruments sponsors some research at York College. The arrangement frankly sounds good to me, good for both parties. York College needs the research funds and is exceedingly happy to have them. Wooley apparently wants the research results because they're of value to its product development effort. York retains the privilege, according to the contract, of publishing the research, as an academic institution must insist it be allowed to do."

"Yes, and moreover, Stan, York College will own all patents that may result. Also, Stan, in consideration of Wooley Instruments Corporation's generosity in furnishing the research money, Wooley is granted a royalty-free license under the patents. Other corporations will have to pay license fees to York College."

"It all sounds fair to me, Sid. But how can I be sure — when the same attorney represented both sides?"

"But were the two parties antagonists, Stan? Certainly not! Both the company and the college were trying to help each other. The arrangement we made is a common one, applied all over the country, whenever some industrial outfit wants to provide financial backing for a university's research program. Anyway, remember, Stan, that you, as the president of York, will always review every proposed agreement. You, not the attorney, are the one who will make the decision as to whether any arrangement is good for York College."

"But suppose I am also a director of Wooley. Then I have an equal obligation to seek the best deal for Wooley. I'll be working simultaneously for both sides of the negotiation, will I not — if I go on the Wooley board?"

"Stan, my philosopher friend, I'm a lawyer. Let me tell you that, very often, two parties in negotiation turn to a third party, usually an attorney mutually chosen, to act as referee or agent in bringing them to a final deal. The two parties to the negotiation choose to trust one and the same individual to have both of their separate interests in mind and to construct the best deal fair to both. Both Wooley

Instruments and York College will expect you, Stan, as do I, the attorney for both, to look for the best, fairest arrangement."

"I hear what you're saying, Sid. So — can we turn now to Wooley Instruments' legal liabilities — the court actions now pending against it? You mentioned earlier that there are at present a dozen or so suits. What's the worst suit? I guess I mean which case, if lost, would cost the company the most? Which case might be most likely to cause the shareholders to blame the directors and sue us?"

"Alright, let's get to that, Stan. First of all, Wooley Instruments has directors' liability insurance. We pay a handsome sum annually for it. The insurance company will take the loss, not the directors personally, if a case goes against us and monetary damages are assessed against the directors by the court or as a result of an out-of-court settlement."

"Aside from the money liabilities, Sid, might not the company and its directors be accused of violating some laws? Might there not be some danger of jail sentences for directors?"

"Stan, now you're talking about something else again. The directors' liability insurance doesn't protect the directors — it doesn't pay damages granted to others or fines imposed by a court — if the directors have actually committed crimes. But you aren't going to commit any crimes. We don't have criminals on the Wooley Instruments' board of directors."

"But what if I don't realize I'm violating the law? There are so many legal complications involved in running a corporation. As a director I'll be asked, won't I, to sign lots of documents. I won't know if all the facts in those documents are correct. How could I possibly always know? What if, say, I should become inadvertently a party to misinforming the government in some way about the corporation? Take just the corporation's income tax filings. Individuals have been jailed for filing a false income tax report, have they not?"

"You would only risk jail for being a party to Wooley Corporation's filing a false tax report if it was your <u>intention</u> to do so. As a corporate director, you do have an obligation to read what you sign. You also are responsible for seeing that the corporation employs what it is reasonable for you to believe are competent legal and accounting experts. If you've seen to that, then the government won't try to put you in jail. Should some bureaucrat out of stupidity or incompetence claim you have purposely, knowingly, misinformed the government, we'll easily beat that."

"Alright, Sid. Now, what's the worst case now pending, if there is a worst?"

"Probably the Lloyd Anderson case. Anderson is an inventor. We tried to hire him at Wooley Corporation. We tried to buy his inventions and put him to work to develop them. But he was interested only in setting up a new company. We finally made a deal. We financed his new start-up company with Wooley Instruments owning fifty percent and Anderson owning fifty percent, this with the understanding that we could buy out his fifty percent interest after five years and merge the new company into Wooley."

"What price would be paid for his fifty percent?"

"The deal, Stan, was that Wooley Corporation and Anderson would each choose an outside price evaluating firm. Those two firms would independently come up with their estimated market value of Anderson's stock. We would then take the average of the two prices and pay Anderson that figure."

"What happened, Sid? Did he think the sale figure too low when he saw it?"

"No. The transaction went through as planned. He took the money, apparently satisfied with the price, and the company was merged into Wooley Instruments. Two years later his wife starts divorce proceedings. Mind you, Anderson got over ten million dollars after taxes and Mrs. Anderson is sure to get half of that in the divorce settlement — community property, you know. But her lawyer claims we cheated Anderson and hence Mrs. Anderson. He argues the price we paid for the stock should have been three times higher."

"Does Mrs. Anderson's attorney have any real case, Sid, any evidence of cheating, or whatever?"

"None at all. That lawyer is a typical shyster. He figures that if he goes after us for several million dollars and threatens to use a lot of the time of Wooley's executives and to generate negative publicity to hurt us, we'll have to give him something substantial because it will be worth it to get rid of him — a cash settlement that he'll probably grab most of as his fee. He's already proposed negotiation rather than going to court. We've said no very firmly. It's a matter of principle to us — even though it would be cheaper to pay him off with a few hundred thousand, which he would probably accept. This is a typical situation. Of course you will not be involved; the key events occurred before you became a director."

"But if I become a director I would be involved, would I not, in deciding whether to settle for some specific sum versus letting it go to court?"

"Not really, only theoretically. Suppose we could settle the case for, say, two hundred thousand. CEO Arthur Wooley and I would decide it and handle it. It would not go to the board for prior approval because it's too trivial an amount of money. It would merely be an information item to the board at the next meeting.

"I noticed, Sid, that Wooley Corporation deals exclusively with Century Independence Bank. That bank holds all Wooley Corporation's cash deposits and checking accounts, and they provide all the working capital loans. Their president, Malcolm Turner, is on the Wooley board, is he not? What if the board wants to consider using a competitive bank to be sure it's paying minimum interest on its borrowings. Wouldn't it be awkward for the board to have a discussion about something like that when Mr. Turner is sitting right there on the board? Not just awkward, in fact. Turner certainly could not be allowed to participate in the decision of which bank to choose. It would be improper for him to hear the pros and cons of continuing with his bank versus shifting to a rival bank. Yet, as a director, he can't be sent out of the room. Legally he is supposed to always be present, to always represent the interests of the shareholders."

"It doesn't work that way, Stan. First, the interest rates for every category of business is virtually the same with all good banks. Next, when it comes to choosing bankers, there's a lot more to it than just getting the lowest interest rate. A long term close relationship is important. You may need a quick loan because something unforeseen comes up, like an opportunity to buy another company where you have to act fast or lose the opportunity. The bank must know your company well. The bank's leaders must know your leaders so they can be confident enough in each other to act quickly."

"But, suppose, Sid, that Wooley Instruments really ought to change commercial banks."

"O.K., Stan, suppose that. The first to know that Century Independence is not doing right by Wooley Instruments would be Arthur Wooley, the CEO, and his financial vice president, Steve Kent. Wooley and Kent would go ahead and choose a new bank. At the next board meeting, the change would be approved by the board. Of course Malcolm Turner would resign from the board."

"Which says to me that Mr. Turner is on the board as much to get Wooley's business for his bank as he is to represent the shareholders, but the latter and that alone is what he is supposed to be doing to his best ability."

"Theoretically, again, my boy."

"And Sid, forgive me, but can Arthur change corporate law firms straightforwardly if one day he becomes unhappy with what he thinks your firm is doing for him?"

"He certainly could. Absolutely! Arthur would just tell me he wants a different attorney, and I'd immediately resign from the board. There would be no problem at all, Stan."

"But you are also Arthur's personal attorney. Don't you ever have trouble sorting out the different interests? Are Arthur's Interests and Wooley Instruments Corporation's interests always in sync?"

"The advantage of having the same attorney cover both the company and its CEO personally is that the attorney can help keep them in sync, as you say. There are potential conflicts, but the worst of those don't begin to negate the advantages. Take the company's contract with Arthur. It covers his base compensation, bonus, termination payments upon retirement, protection should the company be taken over by others — everything. There is a compensation committee of the Board and it employs an outside consulting firm that recommends Arthur's compensation. They do it by studying what the salary ranges are for CEO's of other companies similar in size, profits, nature of business, and so on. The board and Arthur rely on me only to set things down on paper in proper legal form so as to meet all requirements for a clear understanding. It would be clumsy — it would be time consuming, expensive, self-defeating — to have two lawyers, one representing Arthur, the other the company — two lawyers working against each other during the forging of the agreement, each lawyer trying to get for his client some special advantages to justify his fee."

* * * * *

"I'm telling you, Arthur, that it would be a very bad mistake to put this naïve young college president, Stanley Del Mar, with his highly exaggerated and unreal ideas of ethics, on the Wooley board. He doesn't understand anything about how the corporate world works. It wouldn't be so bad if he were passive — you know, inclined to sit back and learn, to depend on his elders for judgments and instructions until he finds his way in the new world he's entering. But he's not built that way. Beneath his soft, gentleman manner, his nice-guy smile and his handsome, "I love people" face, he's intellectually very aggressive. He doesn't really take anyone else's word for anything. He will probably make a great president for York College, but he is an extremist. He will be a troublemaker on any business board. He'll drive you and the other Wooley board members and me crazy with his persistent questioning of every little thing."

"Well — hearing all this about your meeting with him, Sid, I have to agree. Of course, I really don't want him now on my corporation's board. I wish I hadn't invited him, Sid. But I did. After his conversations with you, when you gave him so many strong assurances — you know, he'll think it over, and he'll probably decide to accept. He'll probably be calling me any minute to say so, Sid. So — how do I rescind the invitation?"

"You could tell him that, having heard about his misgivings, you don't think he should be pressed to be on the Wooley or on any corporation board and that the trustees should make that a policy regarding the college's president."

"Yes, I could do that. But then maybe our company won't have the special position we have had in using the scientists at York College to beef up our research and development program. It's been a lot cheaper than our hiring more scientists in our laboratories, what with the lower pay of professors and the almost free staff assistance they get to carry on their work by using students. If York's president is not on our board, some of our competitors could move in at the college."

"With this guy, Arthur, the way he thinks — if he goes on your board — he might even lean over backwards and actually choose to not renew the research arrangement you've had with the college, this precisely because he is on your board. You might lose out to competitors just by making the mistake of putting him into what he will regard as a conflict of interest situation."

"So, Sid, how do I tell him he isn't wanted on the board?"

"That's your problem, Arthur. But you better do it or you'll regret it."

*   *   *   *   *

"And Sid Freeman was so smug about it, Elaine, so arrogant — totally unaware that outside his legal-business world there are other, maybe more ethical, ways of looking at things. He's got lots of polish in expressing himself but no true sense of ethics. Either you do things the way they have been done always in his circle or else you are not of what he thinks of as the real world. He equates ethics to the culture of people like him. Well, I want no part of it."

"Aren't you taking an extreme view of this lawyer, dear? After all, Stan, you really are a complete novice in his world. Imagine — if he were to learn about all the feuding that we know goes on in colleges — department heads and deans always forming cabals to do in some other dean or department head — or what some assistant professors or their spouses will do to get tenure when they're in competition with the other young teachers — or the hypocrisy of the publish or perish pattern of university life."

"Yes, yes, Elaine — or the way the senior professor puts his name first on the scholarly articles those under him author. There are copious examples of shameful university ethics — granted."

"So how would you feel, Stan, if Mr. Freeman mentioned such carryings on, in universities and then accused you of being part of one hellishly unethical mob?"

"Ah, Elaine, but here's the difference: If he said that to me, I'd agree with him. I'd admit that academic life is replete with evidence of human weaknesses. I would say that those of us in leadership positions in academe have a duty to minimize such bad occurrences. We should set good examples. We should reward exemplary behavior and oppose and deter unethical activity when we spot it. We should avoid putting people in positions where they are likely to be tempted, in their own selfish interests, to act in ways they shouldn't."

"And Sid Freeman didn't recognize that he had such responsibilities?"

"No. Elaine. He never once admitted that anything was wrong. Every arrangement I asked him about was unethical on its face, because it created clear conflicts of interest the moment the people were handed their missions. Yet he was confident all arrangements were totally O.K. and advantageous to all parties. He replied to every question of mine in an eloquent, but condescending, manner, making clear right off that my every inquiry was merely the result of my being unaware, unsophisticated, and immature. I have no choice but to decline going on Arthur Wooley's board."

"But Stan, if you turn it down Arthur will be offended. He'll rate you way down — as spoiled, disrespectful, unappreciative, and overly impressed with yourself and your own sense of ethics — egotistical and high and mighty — thinking you're too good for his board. You'll endanger your position in the community and as president of York College. Why don't you simply tell Arthur that in your first year at York you believe you must give all your time to the college? So far as I am able to judge, Arthur is a nice man, Stan. I've gotten to like him. He won't hold it against you if you tell him that."

"Elaine — I can't do that. It's not true."

"Then how will you handle it, Stan?"

"I don't know. I just know I'll have to say no and be honest in saying why I'm saying no."

*   *   *   *   *

"Well, Stan, I understand you had quite a meeting with Sid Freeman the other day. I just called to say that he told me about it and to see if you've thought of any more questions — maybe some you'd like to ask me."

"Thanks for your call, Arthur. Sid was very patient with me, Arthur. He gave me a lot to think about."

"So I gather. Your questions to Sid gave me something to think about too, Stan."

"Well — if we've both discovered that we have something to think about, Arthur, do you think perhaps that should tell us something?"

"You mean, Stan, like maybe we don't need to rush a decision here — whether you do or do not go on the Wooley Instrument board?"

"Exactly, Arthur. We could let that decision simmer a while, if that's not too much of a nuisance or a handicap to Wooley Instruments."

"Let's hold up on it, Stan."

"And, for the time being, Arthur, of course I will not be accepting any other corporate board invitation should one be extended to me. It really makes sense for me to concentrate on being president of York College."

"That sounds O.K. to me — for the time being, Stan."

"Then it's agreed?"

"It's agreed."

Chapter 2: Gender Blender

The problem began several years ago when I promoted a woman, Madeleine Field, to be the general manager of the Software Department. I had been made the head of the entire Computer Division and it was my responsibility and privilege to select my replacement as manager of that department. The parent company passed sixteen billion dollars a year at that time; sales are now over twenty billion. A typical department of the company was about a one billion dollar a year business entity with several thousand employees. Maddy became the first woman executive in the company to be promoted to so high an executive level.

I wasn't trying to prove anything by moving Maddy up. I simply chose the best of the candidates. Every one of the five section chiefs in the Software Department at the time was capable enough to head that Department. But Maddy Field, I was certain, possessed the most outstanding combination of technical breadth, leadership, all-around savvy with people, and imagination. She was a most excellent communicator as well. That was important because all executives at the department manager level had to be involved in keeping both the inside staff and the customers happy.

When I say that appointing Maddy to head the Software Department started the trouble, I am particularly thinking about the morning after I made the announcement. That was when the three other candidates — those who did not get the promotion that went instead to Maddy — asked to see me at once.

Let's start with Ron Davidson because his case was the simplest. Ron came right out and told me that he was not about to report to a woman. "Maddy is good," he said, "but the department is bound to go down in quality because lot's of men feel as I do. They won't work for a lady boss. Is it prejudice? Sure it is. But I don't care what it is, just that it's not for me! There are lots of good jobs for guys with my expertise in software. I'm going to go get one and I wish you luck."

Joe Bryant told me something entirely different. Because he didn't get the promotion that meant to him, he said, that he should take his career endeavors elsewhere. He told me he should have been the one selected for the promotion. So obviously, he concluded, I rate him lower than he rates himself. I asked whether his decision to leave the company had anything to do with his new boss being female and he emphatically said it did not, that he believed strongly that the best should win and gender should not enter. He was quitting, he asserted, because someone else — male or female, he didn't care which — got the promotion and he didn't. He volunteered, however, that not all males were as fair-minded as to women being executives as he was. He told me he knew Ron Davidson was quitting, to take one example, because Ron was not willing to work under a woman.

"If you had given the Department head post to me, Nate," he offered, "you wouldn't be losing me and you wouldn't have lost Ron. You really should ask yourself, Nate, if Maddy Field was enough superior to me that it was worth losing Ron and me just to give the job to Maddy. I'll bet Maddy was surprised to get it. She probably assumed I'd be the one you'd choose."

Matt LaPierre, the oldest section head, close to retirement, said Maddy was a great software expert and

"Thanks for your call, Arthur. Sid was very patient with me, Arthur. He gave me a lot to think about."

"So I gather. Your questions to Sid gave me something to think about too, Stan."

"Well — if we've both discovered that we have something to think about, Arthur, do you think perhaps that should tell us something?"

"You mean, Stan, like maybe we don't need to rush a decision here — whether you do or do not go on the Wooley Instrument board?"

"Exactly, Arthur. We could let that decision simmer a while, if that's not too much of a nuisance or a handicap to Wooley Instruments."

"Let's hold up on it, Stan."

"And, for the time being, Arthur, of course I will not be accepting any other corporate board invitation should one be extended to me. It really makes sense for me to concentrate on being president of York College."

"That sounds O.K. to me — for the time being, Stan."

"Then it's agreed?"

"It's agreed."

manager and he would have no problem working under her. He asked to see me because he wanted to be sure I knew that a problem was likely to build up in the Software Department — or, for that matter in the company as a whole — on the male-female front as more and more women were added.

"You'll have to make the men quit expecting the women who are their equal to go fetch the coffees, if you know what I mean. Actually, Nate, I think that on the average the girls are smarter than the boys. I'm personally too old to care, but you better know you're going to have a gender problem, and you better think a lot about how to handle it," said Matt.

But all that was some years ago. Things are a bit different now. In the Software Department about half of the new recruits from the universities are now women. But gender blending is still not perfect anywhere in the entire company, as was confirmed for me last week when the big boss, Alex Bond, the parent company's Chairman of the Board and CEO, the founder of the company, called me in for a chat. He told me — and directed me to keep it confidential — that my direct superior, the President and Chief Operating Officer, has just discovered he has a serious heart problem and is resigning soon. Alex announced that I was the leading candidate to be the new President.

"Except for one issue about you that the board and I are worried about," said Alex. "It has to do with your possibly overly intensive interest in promoting women into management posts. You've done it far more than any of the company's other top executives. I know, Nate, that you do it because you simply choose the best person, irrespective of gender, to fill the opening. And in computers — at least in computer software — there are lots of very outstanding ladies who are fully deserving of promotions to the higher executive posts. But there is still plenty of prejudice, Nate, on the part of men about working under women. And there is more — like last week a complaint, in the form of a mere suggestion, reached me from some men employees — I'm talking about technical guys, engineers and scientists — about not allowing pregnant women to go on working here in the later months of pregnancy when they get so bulky and awkward and slow moving and are always leaving meetings abruptly, you know, to go to the lavatories, and that sort of thing."

"Specifically," I decided to ask Alex, "You want to know whether, if I'm moved up to President, I might propose a woman to replace me as head of the Computer Division. Is that it?" I asked.

"Well, we can start with that," replied Alex. "I'll bet you have a name already in mind — maybe Madeline Field."

"No, Alex," I replied, "not Maddy. She's terrific, but that's for software, which she manages so well. She hasn't any hardware and overall computer design experience. No, I would recommend a particular person in the Systems Department."

"Let's see" replied Alex. That maybe would be Aimee Jones, Dr. Jones, that you made the manager of the Systems Department not too long ago. Am I right?"

"Yes," I answered.

"A lady," said Alex.

"A great lady and a top executive," I replied.

"We can't have you do that," said Alex, one word at a time, slowly, emphatically, and grimly.

"Would you tell me why?" I asked, not having expected his quick bluntness and so a bit taken aback by it. "I mean is it because you don't share with me the belief that Aimee is the best choice or is it just because she's a woman?"

"You put a woman in as head of our Computer Division," replied Alex, "and you'll lose a number of key department heads who are men and who would not want to report to her and whom you know well our competitors would love to hire away. Tell me, Nate, why can't you be satisfied to be <u>almost</u> perfect — rather than <u>totally</u> perfect — in ruling out gender when you make an appointment? We're running a business so we have to compromise and optimize when we make decisions. Nate, I grant you that ignoring gender is good policy. But holding on to top people is also good policy in our highly competitive business. Those two policies, in the real world, are not wholly compatible with each other. So we are forced to balance things. Probably some years from now males will have become accustomed to working under females just as they're comfortable working under other males. Then there'll be no problem. But today there's still enough of a bias issue that you can't ignore it."

Mind you now, the great Dr. Bond was expressing this prejudice despite knowing that one of our competitors — not the biggest one but the one growing most rapidly and, in my opinion at least, might soon become our biggest rival — is headed by a woman, the dynamic Virginia Rand. Also, I knew, and Alex didn't know, that Ms. Rand had made an offer to me to join her as President of her company, reporting, of course, to her as Chairman of the Board and CEO. Moreover he couldn't know that I was considering the offer seriously. This was not because the compensation — salary, bonus, and stock options — was so attractive, which it was. You know, I happen to be from a financially independent family. No, it was because I had become highly impressed with Virginia Rand as a leader.

Then the high and mighty Dr. Bond went on to bring up one more thing, one suggesting to me immediately that he and I were farther apart than I had fully realized. He asked "How is your mother, Nate? Is she still active?"

That question was the equivalent of saying to me that I inherited from my mother my exceptional interest in treating the female gender fairly. My dad and my mom, Paul and Martha Doheny, had founded what became a very successful accounting firm, "Doheny and Doheny." It made them millionaires and brought more millions when my mother sold it a year after my father's premature death from lung cancer. Especially pertinent to Dr. Bond's bringing my mother into our discussion was my mother's rather famous book, "Gentlemen Prefer Gentlemen." It was a best seller business book some years back and is still frequently cited. It was cleverly written with much wit but was a very serious book about business being a man's world, difficult for women to fully penetrate.

My parents met at the University of Southern California where both received degrees in accounting the same year. Martha was at the top of the class while Paul was in the middle but with an especially attractive personality. Paul immediately landed a job after graduation with a top accounting firm and Martha had difficulty getting good offers, just as did the other female accounting graduates. She finally went to work for a small (three-man) accounting group.

My parents married right after graduation. Paul advanced rapidly and Martha took evening law courses that led to her passing the bar exam on the first try and becoming expert in tax law. In a few years, Paul decided they should start their own firm. He lined up the clients, many small businesses in the Los Angeles area, while Martha led the efforts internally and their firm grew rapidly. (They also raised two children, neither interested in accounting. Sister Janice began selling her unusual paintings while in high school and I, Nathaniel, was a computer enthusiast.) When Paul died, Martha became head of the firm and so began to deal directly with the heads of the client companies, all of whom were men.

Because of dinner discussions, my sister and I, from the time we were teenagers, knew very well about how some men in a business felt about women in the firm and how careful you had to be when you put men in a position where they would have to take orders from a woman. We understood that in their firm it was my mother who had the big brains. She ensured that the clients' accounting and tax law needs were cared for in a most effective way, their taxes minimized, their discretionary accounting decisions made optimally for the running of their businesses, and their accounting data systems designed for accuracy, completeness, and efficiency. Dad's job was more to ensure that the clients, all headed by men, were happy.

Within less than a year after Dad's death, it became clear to my mother that Doheny and Doheny should be sold. That was better than to assign some man to take from my mother the title of President of the firm that my dad had used and that my mother assumed upon his death. (Once a year, when the contract was renewed with each client, a celebratory afternoon with golf was indicated closing with a dinner at the club — the men drinking and eating together and telling a few jokes, some about women, some about women executives — a good old boys relaxing session. My mother arranged for the firm's men vice-presidents to handle those occasions.) The men clients, however, wanted to deal directly with the man at the top — man to man. That is why my mother was certain the clients would soon begin not to renew their contracts with Doheny and Doheny. Better sell out for a good price to a big national firm while the client list and the income were still intact.

Now you can probably see why, after much thinking during the rest of the day at the office following the meeting with Alex Bond, I came home to announce to my wife, Joyce, that I had decided to take the offer from Virginia Rand. The look on Joyce's face told me right away that she didn't like it. She questioned whether that was wise, whether I wouldn't regret leaving RTI, whether reporting to Virginia Rand would be as pleasant for me as reporting to Alex Bond.

"Dr. Bond's right, you know," Joyce said. "You do have to avoid pretending women don't have a handicap when they are in posts where success depends on men taking orders from them."

Then, after a little more conversation, something else important that I had not thought about suddenly popped up.

"I don't want you to be reporting to and working under Virginia Rand." Joyce finally said it.

I foolishly tried being funny. "Don't tell me, Joyce, that you're jealous — because she's a glamour gal — or so the media makes out. You're much prettier," I said "and I love you. I won't fall for her," I said, smiling hard, but actually now troubled as I said it.

"I'll tell you what I think it is, Nate," she responded. "I'm *the* woman — I'm the *only* woman in your life. But, you go to work for her and I don't care how huge the company gets because of the team of her and you, and how successful and important you may get to be as its president. She will be your boss. She will be with you a good part of most days. She is bound to differ with you at times. She'll criticize you when she wants you to be different — you know, like a wife. You'll be thinking about how to please her — how to change so you will — whether to apologize if you said something wrong. When you come to bed you'll have something on your mind about her — what you should do about the next day with her. You'll be spending much more time with her than with me. You'll do luncheons to prepare for a meeting — do business dinners with customers where I would not be present and should not be.

"You'll have *two* women in your life. I'll be one of two, not *the* woman in your life. It would be bound to be that way. Nate, look, if you don't like working for Alex Bond anymore, then go somewhere else. Or start your own company. Your dad did it. You've got the money to do it. But I don't want you to go to work for Virginia Rand."

So I stayed at RTI. I'm the new president there. And I'm now being careful about striving for absolute equality for each of the two genders.

Chapter 3: The Karman Kar

Fritz Karman's repair shop, where Thomas Evers took his autos for maintenance, specialized in Porsches. Tom's cars required substantial attention because he wanted them always to be perfect. Speeding with an eye out for cops was his only hobby. Tom and Fritz formed a personal attachment early despite their great differences in background and a fifteen-year age gap. They fell into the pattern of engaging in long conversations about cars whenever Tom brought a car in. Fritz did not mix in big business circles, of course, but he knew about Tom's high stature in the industrial world and his wealth, which Fritz figured was beyond that of any of his other rich clients.

One day Fritz confided to Tom that he was working on an auto invention and he invited the celebrated inventor and entrepreneur to come look at it. The time chosen for the demonstration was a sunny Sunday afternoon. Into the large lot behind his shop Fritz pushed out a bodiless chassis — four wheels on a metal frame, equipment here and there, a steering wheel, some pedals, and a single seat of sorts.

"This is a prototype, a skeleton for a new kind of car, Tom. It will be more economical to operate, last longer, pollute less, and it'll be a lot quieter and smoother than any car on the market."

"I doubt that very much, Fritz. I see a batch of batteries here. We know battery operated cars are not really good. If you're going to need an internal combustion engine anyway then why all the batteries? Right off, your great idea has the bad parts of both electric and gas autos, I'm guessing. You better stick to repairing cars, Fritz. Remember, I'm both an engineering genius and a business genius and I say forget it."

Fritz managed half a smile briefly in response to what he regarded as Tom's failed effort to be funny but Fritz remained intent.

"Here, Tom, sit down. Turn the key. OK, now — see this engine right here? Hear it? It's hard to hear it isn't it? Well, that engine is not idling. Nope. It's running at full speed and power output. If we were to let all its power go to the wheels, it would have you moving at 35 miles an hour."

"But I'm sitting here dead still. So, Fritz, I naturally wonder where all this engine's generated full power output is going -- if it's not going to the wheels — as if I couldn't guess, seeing all these batteries."

"Yes, Tom, the power of that engine is now turning an electric generator that's right here next to the engine. It's producing electricity that's charging the batteries. Look at this ammeter here on the dashboard. Yes, that's a dashboard. See, it says 'Charge' — and see that reading, all those amperes? They're all flowing into the batteries. I'm going to get on and crouch behind you. Now, press your foot down a little on the accelerator, very carefully, and we'll start to move. This is a pretty big area here, but I don't want you to get up much speed. Just circle slowly.

"I called this unit the electric generator, but it's actually a very tricky, complex device. I'm really proud of it. It's an amazing combination that sometimes acts as an electric motor, sometimes an electric generator, and sometimes a fluid flow clutch, with a bunch of semi-conductor electronics to control it. I call it an 'Electroclutch.' It gets into the act when you step on the accelerator. Now we're moving because some of the power from this little engine is going by way of the Electroclutch directly to the wheels. Look here — notice that the reading on the ammeter has diminished. The batteries are still being charged, but less now, because the car's motion is using up some of the power."

"OK, Fritz, so we're moving now. I'm not going to press down more on the accelerator. I'm not going to go out on the street with this pile of junk. How fast will this thing go?"

"First, Tom, let me tell you that if you were to accelerate up to 35 miles an hour, and hold it there, on level terrain — at that speed, the ammeter would read zero, meaning —"

"Meaning that at 35 miles an hour," replied Tom, "all of the gasoline engine's power would be going into the wheels. The batteries would be getting none of it then, correct?"

"Correct. Tom, just pull up over here and we'll talk a minute. Say you're out on the freeway and want to go 60 — then, naturally, you just press the accelerator down more. Then the Electroclutch will make the batteries give out some of their stored energy and the Electroclutch will act as an electric motor adding torque to the little engine's always constant output and that will get you up to the 60 miles an hour."

"OK, I get it, Fritz," said Tom, now with a totally interested look on his face, "but why is it so great? Why is it so economical and cheap and so light on air pollution?"

"First of all," replied Fritz, "that engine is the first auto gasoline engine to run always at a constant power and speed. It's either totally off — or else it's running at full output — nothing in between. From the very moment you turn it on, whether you're still at the curb or whether you're accelerating or decelerating or going 25 miles an hour or 50 miles an hour — I don't care what speed — this little engine always runs at that same RPM and power output. As you know, of course, an internal combustion engine is not the greatest thing in the world for speed changes. When you make it change speed you have to alter the fuel flow and the air flow and the ignition timing and everything else. It gets inefficient and it pollutes a lot."

"Fritz, don't bother me with these technical details. So you save some fuel and you can leave out some parts when you produce power out of this gasoline engine. You tune it, you perfect its design, for that one condition. And that's a lot better in every way than if the engine has to constantly adjust to all kinds of speed and power conditions."

"Yep. You're catching on, Tom. Besides, this car will never waste energy in traffic when you're standing still and idling or just crawling along. The energy from the engine will then all go into the batteries and be stored there. But there's more. I use electric braking. I mean, that when you press the brake pedal, the Electroclutch becomes an electric generator. It acts as a load, hence as a brake, as it takes the car's forward energy and puts it into the batteries, instead of heating up brakes. Aside from saving fuel, no brakes is a lot cheaper than brakes. There's nothing to wear out — no brake linings."

"But batteries are heavy and have a short life and you can't go far without having to have them recharged. That's what's always been wrong with electric cars."

Tom already knew how Fritz would respond to that remark, but he simply could not resist playing the low savvy provocateur with his sober young friend.

"Don't you see, Tom? In this car the batteries are small and light because they do not have the job of getting you anywhere. They just go up and down in their charge. They're almost always nearly fully charged. If you're traveling at less than 35 miles an hour, or braking, say, then they're being charged. If you're going above 35 miles an hour, or accelerating, then they're being discharged. These batteries just take care of the energy differences required in driving."

"You should say, Fritz, that all of the energy you use comes from the gasoline engine, none of it from the batteries. When you don't need all the energy the engine produces, you store it in the batteries. It's like putting surplus money in a bank account. You withdraw stored energy from the batteries when you need extra power just as you take cash out of a bank account to pay bills. The bank account doesn't create money. You put money in and you take it out."

"OK, genius. Anyway, you see, I've got a whole collection of inventions on this thing and —"

"And I'll bet you haven't filed for a single patent. Well, Fritz, the first thing we've got to do is put you together with a couple of good patent attorneys and get the patents filed. Then we've got to assign you some hot production engineers who can figure out how best to get this Karman Kar produced in quantity. We've also got to have design concepts for the body, something really attractive, exciting, and unique, both inside and out. Then we're going to have to consider how this thing can be marketed and distributed. And how we're going to get the money to build assembly plants so we can mass produce to sell Karman Kars to enough people all over the world to get the price down."

"I've got some questions, Tom. Where's the money going to come from to do all these things you're talking about — the patent attorneys, the production engineers?"

"From me, Fritz, as though you hadn't already planned it. Next question."

"You called this thing a Karman car?"

"Yes, Karman Kar — spelled with a K — K-A-R. Karman Motors — that'll be the name of the company we're going to launch — to make and sell a new, small, runabout car — a get-to-work car, a shopping car, a teenagers' car, a car for the daily needs of most city drivers — and the inventor is a guy by the name of Karman. The name, Karman Kar, with the two nice hard Ks, sounds right to me. It's a natural. Remember, Fritz, I'm putting up the money, I'll choose the name."

And they shook hands. During the following year Karman Motors spent several million dollars furnished by Tom, making and testing Electroclutches and assembling two complete prototype chassis with no bodies, although a couple of designers came up with some attractive novel body design ideas.

Tom proposed that to minimize capital needs the new company should not build factories to make parts. The components, even the parts of the Electroclutch and the car's body pieces, would all be obtained from competitive independent automotive parts manufacturers in the U.S., Japan, Korea, Mexico, and maybe China and India. However, there had to be assembly facilities, servicing centers, training programs for maintenance mechanics, and an efficient world supply system for spare parts. All the selling and customer service would be handled by existing automobile dealers, Tom estimated that $200 million of start-up capital would be required. That was big enough to mean to Tom a stock offering to the public preceded by presenting a detailed business plan to the right Wall Street firms.

Tom and Fritz began spending evenings working out all these plans in the study at Tom's elegant home. Then they shifted to Fritz's little house instead where, before starting work, they would eat a simple supper prepared by Fritz's young wife, Marlene. Tom was immediately taken with young Marlene. Fritz had discovered and quickly married her in Germany while on a U.s. Army Reserve hitch. She was now twenty years old, had a little daughter just learning to walk and was pregnant again, so Tom was told, although he would not have guessed it from noting what he judged to be a perfect and seductive figure. The child was redheaded like her father, but fortunately for her she resembled very much more her very beautiful blond mother and, like her, was all smiles and affection.

As soon as dinner ended, Tom and Fritz would cover the dining room table with papers full of sketches, numbers, and lists and pour over them. The little girl, late in being put to bed the first night Tom was there, kept crawling to Tom and pulling herself up on his pants legs. At one point Tom had not been able to resist picking her up and touching her cheeks to his. He had never held a tot close before and it felt good. Tom thought how wonderful it would be to be like Fritz, to have a loving wife and children, and do things for them, and bask in the warmth of intimate family relationships — something he had never known. Since his young wife's and expectant child's deaths in an airplane accident and a short second marriage ending in divorce, he had been a bachelor. Now into his forties, he was possessed of enormous wealth but had no one he really cared about to spend it on or eventually leave it to.

Later, in one evening at Fritz's home, Marlene, who had served them coffee, came up to Tom from behind his chair, surprised him with her lips hard on his brow, and then ended the embrace with a loud kiss on it. She asked, "Fritz and me, Tom — are we going to be rich? Fritz says yes. I would love that."

"Yes, Marlene, you and Fritz are going to be rich," Tom replied.

Tom's prediction was not totally wrong for Marlene, as it turned out, but it was for Fritz, who, through a series of misjudgments, managed to lose his company, a potential fortune, and his self-respect. Marlene's trust fund, a gift from Tom, was both the result of and a contribution to Fritz's mistakes and consequent misfortune.

Tom worked out the financing with investment capital sources. But, as the arrangements for a public stock sale were being finalized, Fritz showed what was to Tom a surprising antagonism to anything that Tom had to say. At the last moment, with the new company about to receive the funds to implement the plan they had worked out together, Fritz totally rejected the deal. He was afraid, he said, that they would lose control of their company to "the big financiers." Besides, he announced, he had decided Tom's money estimates were too high.

"Nowhere near $200 million is needed. You and I now hold all the stock. If we go to Wall Street, then our percentage, instead of being fifty percent each, will soon go down to practically nothing. We won't have control anymore."

"Fritz," answered Tom, "the deal, as you and I have gone over at length, is that almost all of the $200 million of financing will be in the form of preferred stock and bonds, with the sale of only 50 percent of the common stock. We'll still each end up with twenty-five percent of the common. Our combined fifty percent of all common shares will control any widely held corporation and the plan is for the other fifty percent of the common and all of the preferred and all the bonds to be sold nationwide in small blocks through a thousand brokers. If we do a good job of running the company, the owners of the other fifty percent can be counted on to back us up on everything. I know this game. Only if the company is headed for failure and more cash is desperately needed to avoid bankruptcy could the company's control slip away from us. That's a chance we should take. You shouldn't be so afraid we're going to fail."

"It's you, Tom, that's afraid of failure," Fritz shouted. "That's why you want so much money available. We're not going to need factories for parts, just to assemble them. I say we can hold on to all the shares and just borrow money as we need it. With all the good publicity we've gotten already there are plenty of people who will gamble on us."

"Fritz, be realistic. People who gamble want to see a chance of a big gain in return for their big risk. They'll want shares of the company. You couldn't offer a high enough interest rate to get the money through loans alone. Hell, I could put up the money myself, but we want a large number of owners, to help put this new auto over with the public. We've decided all this together — the two of us, Fritz."

When Tom found that Fritz was immovable, increasingly emotional, irrational, and, especially, unfriendly, he decided there was no alternative but to bow out and leave the company to Fritz to run any way he wished. Fritz appeared anxious to acquire Tom's shares so he could have the full one hundred percent ownership, Tom proposed that Fritz, as long as he was planning to borrow many millions, should borrow another $10 million from his backers and buy Tom's shares. Fritz, enraged, said $10 million was too high a price.

"Fritz, for hell's sake," Tom responded, "in the deal I had all set, Wall Street was prepared to sell shares at a price equivalent to our own shares having a value of $50 million each. The $10 million I'm asking is way below the true market price, don't you see?"

Finally, disappointed in and disgusted with Fritz's reaction to what Tom knew was an enormously generous offer, and anxious to terminate a relationship that Fritz had strangely turned into a severely unpleasant one, Tom accepted $5 million.

Fritz succeeded in arranging to borrow $25 million by going after all the rich customers of his foreign car service garage, but that required him to pledge all of his stock in the company as security. Tom knew Fritz was seriously low in estimating both the needed start-up capital and the company's operating expenses. Also, by underestimating the cost to produce them, he was under-pricing the vehicles. The loan agreement said that if the company did not break even by the third year, or could not meet the interest payments then, the backers could foreclose. Tom now was certain that Fritz's financial backers soon would have all his stock. Fritz then would have nothing.

With his high personal net worth and his concern about Marlene and her children, Tom took the 5 million dollars, added 5 more, and set up a $10 million trust fund for Marlene and her offspring, paying the gift taxes himself. Marlene would receive only the income to use as she pleased until her children became adults, at which time she could withdraw the capital to herself as she wished.

Tom had dropped in at Fritz's home to tell him and Marlene about the trust fund, first phoning her to be sure they were home. Tom thought his announcement of the trust fund, a clearly friendly gesture which should be a marvelously happy surprise to them, together with Fritz's pleasure at now having one hundred percent of the company, would so please Fritz that whatever had come between them would now evaporate. Instead, when he arrived, he was treated to a tirade by Fritz, with Marlene standing by helplessly.

Unfortunately, when Marlene had approved Tom's coming over, she had not known that Fritz had invited a news reporter to announce the financing he had arranged and the schedule for production of his new automobile. From the adjacent room where they had been meeting and which Fritz left for a moment when Tom arrived, the reporter had overheard Fritz telling Tom loudly that he "did not need his money or his friendship." Tom, so perplexed that he said nothing in response, left hurriedly.

The next day a piece appeared in the newspaper saying that Messrs. Karman and Evers, the two original partners of Karman Motors, had had a falling out, that Karman was now the sole owner of the company, and also that Evers had set up a 10 million dollar trust fund in Mrs. Karman's name. The article noted that Thomas Evers was an extremely wealthy man and a bachelor.

That evening Tom's houseman told him that there was a lady at the door. Tom found Marlene Karman standing there.

"I came to explain, Tom," said Marlene, looking troubled but beautiful.

"Come in, Marlene — then tell me what you came to explain."

She stepped in and suddenly threw her arms around him and hugged him closely. Awkwardly, he put his arms around her in turn, puzzled and concerned.

"Well," he said, still holding her, "what's this all about?

"Fritz was filthy nasty to you."

"That's for sure. And damned if I know why."

"I know why, Tom."

"Then tell me!"

"He thinks we're lovers," she murmured quietly.

Tom pushed her away in a quick reaction.

"What! No! Why in the — ? Did you tell him right away that we aren't? We've never even been alone! Did you straighten him out?"

"Sure. I told him. But he wouldn't believe me. Then he asked me to deny you were attracted to me."

He stared, aghast, fearing her next words.

"I told him you were." She looked at Tom plaintively.

"No! You didn't! Marlene! What's the matter with you?"

"I know you don't love me, but you like me — and you want me. I know from the way you look at me — and Fritz — he's seen it too."

"Oh, God, Marlene! Go home — go take care of your husband and your little girl — go, go — now!"

Karman Motors survived two more years. During that time Fritz obtained additional financing, surrendering more and more of his stock with each extension. A first batch of Karman Kars were produced and sold but all had trouble with a critical component, the Electroclutch. It malfunctioned too often. Fritz finally was fired by the outside directors. He had given them his last shares in the company and had also to sell his garage to partially settle his debt. The company filed for bankruptcy. Now he had no job and no personal funds.

Tom became increasingly unhappy as he saw what was happening to Karman Motors and Fritz Karman. As a consequence of the trust fund Tom had created, Marlene and her children and, of course, Fritz himself, would have an assured income that the company's creditors could not touch. Tom was thankful that he had been wise enough to put the trust in Marlene's name, even as he was sorry he had not anticipated the way Fritz would react and thus had unwittingly exacerbated Fritz's animosity.

Tom felt certain that the failure of the Karman Kar need not and indeed would not have occurred had his partnership with Fritz not broken up. Was the blame his? He knew he had mourned the death of his sweetheart and his unborn child too long and that in recent years he had come to miss and yearn for female companionship. He had not realized, however, until this situation with Fritz and Marlene had exposed it, that he was capable of being — he apparently had become — an ogler of attractive women. How horrible, he thought, if the ladies at his company all saw him as Marlene had, engaging in such loathsome activity as lustful leering. He was unaware he was doing it. Should he seek out Fritz and try to convince him he had never coveted his wife? Could he make Fritz see that his glances, no matter how annoying, were completely innocent and forgivable?

After much pondering, Tom decided on a plan of action. He would buy from the court appointed bankruptcy trustee the full exclusive rights to Karman Kar. He would go to Fritz and offer to put money behind the further developing of the Electroclutch, to make it a truly reliable piece of equipment. Fritz and he, friends again, would re-launch the Karman Kar.

As Tom was about to propose this plan to the trustee, Fritz was desperately mulling over his situation, his and his family's dependence on the income from his wife's trust created by Tom Evers. It never occurred to him to seek out Tom Evers. Instead he decided to drive his car at very high speed off a high coastal road onto the rocks far below.

Chapter 4: Dwarfius

When Robert Curtis was seven years old — a short, fat, excruciatingly shy little boy — his father, a U.S. State Department economist assigned to Geneva, placed him in a Switzerland school. This was just after Robert's mother and his might-have-been sister both died from surgery complications of a premature birth. The teachers in that school soon found Robert far above his classmates intellectually be the subject mathematics, languages, geography, or history. During that first year, he was promoted several times as the faculty tried to locate him with students at his intellectual level. That frequent shifting would have been enough to limit his popularity with the other students, but they made school life difficult for him mainly because they laughed at how he looked.

A few of them also were plump and some were also short for their ages. One was freakishly tall and skinny, a real string bean. But Robert possessed a giggle provoking form, an egg-like body on short legs. When he was brought into the room of the seven year olds on his first day, his classmates began uncontrollable chuckling, a ceremony repeated several times that first year as he was progressively moved to the classes of the eight, nine, ten, and finally the eleven year-olds.

Awareness that his physical appearance was amusing dominated Robert's early school years and afflicted him with extreme self-consciousness. Yet, somehow, by his teenage years, Robert acquired the skill to present a variety of personalities at will. His being an introvert was inherent while the requirement on occasion was to be outgoing, maybe even effusive. So, having pondered the differences in detail, he even could act the part of an extravert. He knew he was considered funny looking and that classmates would laugh him off, either literally or in their minds, on first contact. But Robert also came to realize he was so bright and intellectual that they would notice that fact not too much later and would be forced to take him seriously as a person. His shyness, that means, did not stand in the way of his studying others and learning how to manipulate them when he saw a need. He was analytical down to the very last one of the billions of neurons in his brain. Thus, starting when a child, he became skillful in understanding what was going on about him and to use that understanding to strategize so as to achieve carefully chosen objectives. Robert is still doing that now at age thirty-seven.

By his twelfth year, fully established academically as a prodigy, he was accepted for entry by a small but highly rated college favored by American and English families living in Vienna, Robert's father then having been reassigned to that U.S. embassy. The economist wanted his son to live with him during his early teen years instead of being off on his own among much older students at some university in the United States thousands of miles away. That gave Robert the opportunity to get to know his father well, something that would not have been possible later, what with his father's developing heart problems. Robert learned that his dad was blessed with impressive intellectual potential but had developed no more than a small portion of it. Robert resolved not to allow that to happen to him. Had he not spent those years with his dad, Robert might never have made such a commitment.

Robert received his first college diploma at age fifteen, summa cum laude, with a major in science. He was the youngest graduate in the college's history. He also was the valedictorian that day. As he walked to the podium to deliver his talk, he sensed that he had passed a milestone important to him because it appeared no one seeing him for the first time that afternoon was giggling. At an even five feet tall, he was perceived at that moment merely as much younger and shorter (and plumper) than the other graduates. He was being viewed as a marvel and much more of a curiosity in the brainpower category than in his appearance, though the latter abnormality was still an attention attracter.

After a few paragraphs into his address — which he delivered standing on a six inch pedestal provided just for him — the content of what Robert had chosen to say, the first half in German, the second in English, and the creative way he expressed it took command of the audience. Even as he realized he was being greatly admired for that performance, he recognized he could not much longer get by as the precocious youngster. As he approached being an adult, he would need to possess a very high and very evident mental stature. His mind's brilliant luster would have to force his body's negative characteristics into the background.

Just after the graduation ceremony Robert's father was forced to take early retirement because of his declining health, emphysema having joined heart disease as a serious life-ending threat. He needed the best possible climate for his remaining days. Possessing little more than his modest pension, Robert's father could not fund his son's continuing education. But that was not a problem. Robert's scholastic achievements guaranteed generous scholarships from top universities in America. His dad chose Palo Alto, California, where Stanford's law school offered Robert tuition and living expenses.

Robert entered but found boring the study of law. More specifically, he despised the homework, the reading of cases and more cases. For Robert, too much memorizing was associated with this effort and not nearly enough fascinating application of logic and imagination, this despite the claims of the law professors to the contrary. He could almost instantly spot the issues the Profs wanted the students to be ready to discuss at the next class session. In fact, for every important legal principle the faculty expected would be disclosed by the literature they wanted the students to pore over, Robert could easily spot more.

Unlike the tedium the required mass reading engendered, the class sessions interested and entertained Robert. Here for him were live players: the professors, conceited and sharp, and the students, also conceited and sharp in their own youthful way, each group determined to do in the other. He assumed the action played out in class to be typical of the attractive part of legal activity, namely, skill and originality in scheming to outmaneuver the opponents.

Robert decided that he did not want to become a lawyer. Were it not for the fact that he could read and understand three or four times faster than the other law students, he would have dropped law school very early. But his speed and ease of comprehension enabled him to get top grades in law classes while simultaneously exploring another academic field. The Deans at Stanford indulged this young genius, allowing him to register for enough graduate economics courses that, by also taking summer classes in the subject, it qualified him for a Ph.D. in economics to be awarded when he produced a satisfactory research thesis.

Though Robert planned not ever to practice law, passing the bar became for him a must. In his last year he attended most of his last law classes, found the time to produce an exceptional doctorate thesis in economics, and crammed for the bar exam. That spring he scored very high in his law class exams, passed the California bar, defended his economics thesis, and received two degrees, Doctor of Jurisprudence and Doctor of Philosophy in Economics.

Robert judged no factor more important in choosing what to do next than his "girl" problem. One summer, when he was sixteen, Robert had won a trip to attend an international colloquium for high scholarship college students on the French Riviera. For twelve summer days the young awardees were guests on a luxurious yacht owned by the wealthy university trustee who had funded the project. As they went in and out of yacht harbors, Robert noticed that aboard the expensive pleasure craft docked nearby, beautiful young women could often be seen in the company of old and ugly men. Various readily observable details suggested they were also all very rich men. Some of the girls were much taller than their partners. Robert concluded that a simple rule applied: the further away from being handsome he is the richer a man must be to rate luscious females. Since Robert planned not to allow his body's contour to keep him from enjoying the opposite sex, it followed he needed to become rich. Since he was both short and fat he had to become very rich. And he felt a need to do it soon. That meant he should seek a job involved with handling money — big money — and learn how to capture a good deal of it for himself.

But Robert's father's health became the determining factor. A bad heart attack occurred a month after the son's new university degrees were awarded. The father was now having serious trouble with his breathing and the doctors estimated he had less than a year. So Robert needed a job nearby. Fortunately, Professor Allen Hamilton, under whom Robert had done his economics thesis, was leaving to take the chief executive's post in a Palo Alto semiconductor company, Palotek Corporation. Hamilton offered Robert a job to perform analyses of the European market for Palotek's products. Hamilton told Robert he thought his company "ought to sport at least one authentic genius." Robert winced when he heard that comment, but the job served his temporary situation and he grabbed it.

Robert planned that after losing his father he would find a Wall Street job followed by his launching some sort of get-rich-quick strategy. He would learn at Palotek about the commercial exploiting of new science and technology. He certainly never expected he would stay for four years at Palotek and that he would become a multi-millionaire in that time. It was even farther from his mind that he would choose to become a crook.

In less than a year it became evident to Robert that Palotek was being highly successful in breaking into profitable business in Europe and that that success stemmed entirely from his discoveries and evaluations of specific opportunities for exploiting the company's assets there. Robert instantly became more than a market researcher. Using fully his amazing analytical talents, he judged spectacularly well pertinent technological, economic, social, and political factors. He was innovative as well as investigatory. He conceived of and recommended excellent and concrete deals for the company to implement.

Robert had the main European newspapers sent to him daily. Every six weeks he spent five days in Europe for discussions with European experts whom he identified and then consulted with exceptional cunning. He spoke German like a native and was fluent in French as well. He studied numerous companies in Europe — their markets and technological strengths and the possible benefits to them and Palotek of the right alliances. He pinpointed entrepreneurs who were getting older and tired and should be happy to sell out. Typically those companies became more valuable when Palotek added its products to their lines. He found cities (like Bordeaux in France anxious to expand jobs there beyond wine and into technological products) willing to offer great inducements to American hi-tech companies to create local operations. Moreover, he made out a strong case to predict that the dollar would be seen as overvalued and that acquisitions of foreign companies would cost much more if Palotek delayed, a forecast that soon proved accurate.

Robert did not mix much with others in the company. His communicating with them was virtually entirely through his prolific production of terse memoranda where he explained alternatives and made recommendations for action. Of these writings he was very proud. But, when blocks of Palotek stock were optioned out to about twenty top people in the company, he was not included. Those awards had been determined largely by the size of the staff reporting to the individual. If Robert had had many people working under him, thus placing him in the "executive" category, his salary would have been much higher and his name would have been on the stock option list. It became inconceivable to him — as he was sure it was to Palotek's leaders — that he ever would be placed in charge of an operating sector. He never was going to become an executive at Palotek.

It was only shortly after he arrived there, in fact, that he overheard some crude talk and laughing in the men's lavatory about his body size and shape, most comments having sexual tie-ins thought by the amused commenters to be very funny. Robert knew that that conversation could be considered exceptional only in that he had accidentally overheard it. Sitting and listening, not daring to emerge until they left, he learned he had a nickname, "Dwarfius," their combination of dwarf and genius. People prefer their leaders tall, Robert learned in childhood. The principal executives at Palotek were taller than the average man in the street. Everyone knows there are biases based on color, ethnicity, national origin, religion, and gender, but the discrimination in business corporations against short or fat men in management posts, he knew, to be also real and severe. Robert, possessing both these physical negatives, was slated for the least admired category, one without even the inclusion of a sympathy dimension.

Robert took to daydreaming about making millions and becoming daring in his way of life, particularly during his frequent trips to Europe. He imagined himself with a yacht on the Riviera and his entertaining glamorous women on it. He then reached a key conclusion: Fraud was the easiest and most certain route for him to accumulate wealth quickly. Of course, he could quit his job and play the stock market to advantage since his understanding of economic trends and corporate business finance was well above that of the average stock market investor. But for that strategy to be quickly successful a substantial beginning money stake, which he lacked, was a requirement. Could he found a new company? He would not be credible as a promoter seeking financing for some start-up business that he would propose to head no matter how brilliant, novel, and sound his idea.

His personal efforts were bringing in many millions of dollars annually to Palotek and it could spare him a few million, a sum well below what he felt he deserved. He had simply to devise an approach with a low enough probability of exposure to be acceptable. Anyway, suppose he was caught, he asked himself. Jail he decided would bring him little more distress than the awful feelings of depression he found himself developing when he contemplated the years of frustration and loneliness that loomed ahead.

Robert's father held on to die just before Robert turned twenty-one. He had devoted much of his time the preceding year to attempts at inventing a satisfactory fraud scheme. Then, one morning, out of the blue, Allen Hamilton called Robert into his office. As Hamilton began to talk Robert suddenly realized that the missing link his planning needed for completion was surfacing. Now he knew exactly how to launch his scheme.

Hamilton announced to Robert that he was abandoning Palotek's highly conservative approach to international expansion. Instead of Robert's working alone he would now be given some staff to help plan Palotek's moving all its products aggressively into the entire world market. The company would set up manufacturing plants and sales offices in many countries, buy some offshore companies, negotiate licenses to foreign producers, launch joint ventures with overseas partners, and more. The aim was for Palotek to become a truly multinational company. Robert would have a new title, Director of International Strategy. He would receive a salary increase and would go on the executive's stock option list.

Robert surprised Hamilton by speaking up immediately.

"Since you are displaying such high confidence in me, let me make a suggestion. My work has been accomplished without a staff. I have needed help, of course, but I've gotten it from carefully selected outside consultants, experts in economics, marketing, government, and so on. Some consultants I have used just to make contacts. Some are Americans. Most are foreigners. None have been employed full time on Palotek issues. I call upon them for data, leads, and opinions, but I alone integrate their inputs into the plans I develop. Their expertise has been far superior to what I could have recruited into a permanent staff here and has cost us far less as well.

"Now, for the big international expansion you seek," Robert went on, all of the plotting he had done for a year now piled at the front of his mind ready to be released, "there will be a larger array of different markets to study and many more companies to consider deals with. So I will need more outside consultants. Instead of using here and there three or four I'll need to be in touch with ten or twenty various specialists in the various countries. I'd like to try it that way before going the route of building up a big staff."

Hamilton's eyes lit up. Robert had correctly anticipated that Palotek's chief executive did not relish hiring a large staff for him. Robert had presented not only a lower budget plan, but also one that would eliminate the problem of recruiting people willing to work under him.

"I'll buy that," Hamilton said. "You're right, Robert. It would take a long time to assemble an internal staff as good as the best part-time talent on the outside. But don't go to extremes. If you need a man or two full time on the payroll, hire them."

The first thing Robert then did was to acquire a new secretary. His present one was competent, but security now required his starting anew. When Ms. Reese reported, he described his work pattern. Her hours were to be the usual daytime ones but he said she should know that his would vary greatly. Traveling frequently and having no family obligations, he told her, he often used weekends and evenings to catch up at the office. She was not to be offended if, after hours, he sent off revised e-mails or letters that she might have drafted.

Next, he composed a letter to a number of professionals of considerable prominence — economists, members of leading consulting firms, professors, bankers, investment counselors, former ambassadors, and many others. In this correspondence he asked each recipient to recommend consultants to deal with various specialized areas. The following day he placed in the office computer copies of these memos saying he had sent them personally after hours. Actually he had not communicated any of them.

Especially included in the files were copies of (again un-sent) requests to several especially well-known individuals asking for their comments about a certain consulting firm named Schaeffer and Bonner of Geneva, Switzerland. A week later Robert was off to Geneva where he rented a one-room office in the name of Schaeffer and Bonner. On returning home, Robert created memos for the file describing his visits with various private individuals, companies, and government personnel. He also produced notes regarding a European symposium he had actually attended. Included for the record were reports of fictitious discussions at that symposium with those to whom he earlier had sent letters (presumably, according to his files) asking for their opinions of Schaeffer and Bonner. All of them, his file now showed, had praised these Geneva-based consultants highly.

He then noted, with satisfaction, that the file not only evidenced that he had investigated a substantial number of potential consultants — domestic and foreign — but it recorded his thorough efforts that led to his selection of those consultants he had hired to start his expanded international activities. Schaeffer and Bonner stood at the top of this list. S&B, according to the filed contract with them, were to be paid twenty-five thousand dollars a month and were to make their assistance available through written reports that answered questions to be sent them by Robert. This contract was signed by Charles Schaeffer for Schaeffer and Bonner and by Robert Curtis for Palotek, a committing privilege he now enjoyed in his new higher post.

In the period that followed, Robert e-mailed a report every month from S&B in Geneva to Robert Curtis of Palotek. Each was a remarkable document — particularly when read some months later (after Robert, unbeknownst to his secretary, had revised it, adjusting its predictions to jibe amazingly with actual happenings). Anyone reading the file of past reports would have been enormously impressed with the record of S&B in perceiving correctly ahead of time such things as inflation rates, alterations in the value of the dollar against other currencies, and many specific actions taken by corporations and governments.

Robert had no problem justifying to his file an expanding use of Schaeffer and Bonner and a corollary substantial raising of their monthly fee. As the first year of the arrangement ended and a new one began, S&B's Swiss bank account, what with interest accumulating and the funds always converted immediately to Euros — which Robert had correctly guessed would rise relative to the dollar — was moving rapidly towards the million dollar level.

Meanwhile Palotek's operating executives had ample reason to believe their corporation's international strategy was the best in the business. Robert's analyses were of conspicuous aid to Hamilton and the division managers and Robert's proposals were regularly and speedily implemented. Palotek's foreign business soared. Hamilton raised Robert's salary and bonus and granted him further options on Palotek's common shares. Hamilton and his principal associates now were completely convinced that Robert was indeed a genius who never should be burdened with an operating division manager's job for which he, Dwarfius, clearly would be unsuitable.

Robert would continually re-evaluate the probability of his fraud's being discovered and always concluded it was happily virtually nil. He was highly isolated. He had no accomplices. His files were under his personal tight control. They would look complete and correct should someone examine them, an extremely unlikely possibility. The files would show that Robert had initially justified his use of Schaeffer and Bonner, among other consultants (the rest actual) and that S&B was performing amazingly well.

What if Robert should become ill or be in an accident and someone else should take over his office? The flow of monthly memoranda from Schaeffer and Bonner would then cease. To cover this possibility, Robert placed into the files a letter from S&B stating that they were retiring and that, in accordance with the terms of the contract, they were now giving notice they were terminating it. Each month, Robert re-dated that letter. Thus, if anyone were to enter the file in his absence, that letter would be duly noted and further reports from Schaeffer and Bonner would no longer be expected.

Might someone in the company decide one day to visit S&B in Geneva? This possibility was especially remote because of the very nature of the relationship between Robert and Palotek's other executives. By his never circulating any emails or other records whatsoever from any of his consultants, the Schaeffer and Bonner firm's documents had been nonexistent to everyone in Palotek except for the accounting department. They merely sent monthly checks to Schaeffer and Bonner in response to invoices that Robert was privileged to approve for payment.

Nevertheless, early in the third year, Robert made a stupid mistake of the simplest and careless kind. But, instead of exposure, the accident produced a higher level of revenue into the S&B account.

Joe Collins, a planner from another company that had been involved in a bit of joint activity with Palotek at the time, was paying Robert a visit. Before Collins' arrival, Robert had been on his computer, revising one of the past monthly reports from Schaeffer and Bonner. He amended the display and then accidentally left it on the computer screen. Some time after Collins had arrived Robert stepped out for a few moments. When he returned from the lavatory he was shocked to see that Collins was standing and gazing intently at that computer's display.

"Who are these people, Robert?" Joe asked. "This report is a wonder! Their commentary here on that Europa Electronics outfit — how could they have foreseen what would happen to that company? I remember that Europa Electronics was up for sale and that you and I talked about it. I didn't think their price was too high, Robert, but you did. I didn't know then about their enormous inventory problem that surfaced later, but these Schaeffer and Bonner people apparently did. You bastard! You didn't let on to me that you were getting this kind of information. These guys are good. Who are they anyway?"

"Oh, they're just a consulting firm I use," Robert mumbled while fighting a threat of a heart attack evidenced by the rapid heartbeat banging away ferociously in his ears. "Yes, they're good."

A week later, Collins called Robert to ask if he would object to his company's also using Schaeffer and Bonner's services and how he could get in touch with them. That call Robert had anticipated. He had a ready answer.

"No objection at all. I'll give you their computer address. They work exclusively by answering your specific questions and they communicate entirely electronically. You don't hold phone conversations with them. They don't make detailed research studies that require a big staff.

Rather, they simply render their opinions. They use lots of close personal contacts to seek inside leads and they put a great deal of effort on particular questions where they think they have something valuable to offer. They're sort of like top medical diagnosticians. They don't make house calls, if you know what I mean. Very independent. To contact them, email them some clear questions and ask what they would charge you for answering those questions, to give you their opinions. If they'll take you on, sign them up for a trial year."

The next time Robert went to Geneva, he found email from Collins. Schaeffer and Bonner immediately sent off answers to the questions of this new client. Considering the two hundred and fifty thousand dollars a year fee S&B suggested, and Collins accepted, Robert did not regret the half-hour it had taken for him to prepare an excellent reply to Collins' questions.

Soon S&B built its clientele up to five American corporations, Palotek and four others acquired through word of mouth. The firm was now operating at an annual revenue level of two and a half million dollars and Robert was spending ten days a month in the little Geneva office. Although the fraud then looked perfect from the standpoint of income, he had to assess the danger of exposure as now having grown. So Robert went to Hamilton and told him he was leaving Palotek to accept a position as head of a consulting firm that had offered him a deal of equity and salary that he could not turn down.

Robert suggested to Hamilton that his position in Palotek need not be refilled. Palotek's international business had become very strong, he went on to say, but it still could profit from Robert's advice on the best directions to take for further expansion. He proposed to provide this advice in the future just as he had been doing except that it would be done now through the firm, S&B, he was joining. That firm, Robert explained to Hamilton, was by far the best of all the consultants he had used in the previous years and that his joining them as the head would expand their ability to serve Palotek. Although he would be leaving Palotek, he could assure Hamilton of a service that would be the equivalent of what he had previously supplied and most likely at a lower cost. Hamilton thought all this sounded fine.

In view of the respect Schaeffer and Bonner had earned from its clients, Robert encountered no problems when he told them of his joining the firm as its chief, a firm now to be expanded. He arranged easily for an increased volume of business from each client and then he solicited and signed up with equal ease a number of carefully selected additional corporations. Robert first called the consulting firm Curtis, Schaeffer, Bonner and Associates but later changed it to Curtis Associates and established its head office in New York.

He continued, of course, with his personal conversations with selected individuals in business, government, and the universities, kept up his reading and thinking about big issues and trends, and found it exciting to ponder the questions sent in by his now many clients. Robert's performance received rave reports. All clients judged as spectacular his ability to integrate and distill the detailed data from what they assumed must be a large staff. One principal executive said it well. "From our other outside consultants, we get a big fat report. The data in it are valuable but they mainly relate only indirectly to our decision options. From Robert Curtis, in contrast, we get clear, succinct advice, right to the point -- ideas and understandings we ourselves lack, or at least, don't possess at the same quality level. Robert provides us big advantages over our competitors."

At age twenty-five Robert was netting millions of dollars a year totally legally. By age thirty Robert Curtis had become widely known as one of the top brains of American business. He was sought after as a keynote speaker for major business conventions and began to receive honorary doctorates from leading universities.

His social life changed dramatically. He bought a well-equipped yacht, far from huge but adequately spacious, with a skilled crew of four. He kept it in the Mediterranean and spent time on board thinking, reading, and typing memos to clients — or with women. His wealth gave him confidence with the opposite sex, just as he had guessed it would, and the yacht was an effective aphrodisiac to attractive and adventurous young women.

He saw often a French lady, Monique, whom he met at a Paris dinner party given by a leading banker. She was small and voluptuous, a divorcee five years older than Robert and in most other ways just right. She was five feet three in medium high heels. Not a bad match because Robert in his special shoes became five feet two. Monique's divorce settlement had been substantial but with two children and expensive tastes she was energetically seeking a new rich husband by the strategy and mechanism of sharing her bed with those she regarded as serious candidates. Robert considered marriage but was unwilling to live in Paris as she insisted. She had a weakness for rich desserts and Robert thought she might eventually be shaped like him, which would make for awkwardness under certain important circumstances. So, Robert broadened his consultant practice to help her find and evaluate other prospects for a husband. The consulting fee he charged her was non-monetary but mutually highly satisfactory.

There also was the beautiful London widow, Emily, a prominent antiques dealer. She disdained marriage. She admired Robert's intellect and found him generally so interesting it surmounted her bias regarding their six-inch difference in height. The gap as to this dimension was less noticeable in a horizontal position and actually functionally advantageous because most of the excess height was in her long legs.

Robert did not incur expenses greater than a small fraction of his annual income. He invested the surplus mainly in the right foreign currency, predicting unusually accurately major exchange rate movements before they occurred. The rest of his unneeded income went into the world's stock markets. Here Robert was more fortunate than most speculators in his selections as to when and what to buy and sell. The money in the original Schaeffer and Bonner Swiss bank account grew beautifully through his investment strategy, but nevertheless began to look small compared with Robert's total net worth. He never had been able to invent a way to bring those Swiss S&B funds into the United States under his own name without incurring the attention of tax authorities, with whom he chose not to discuss the matter. He decided he would simply donate that money to a deserving cause at the right time and forego seeking to take a tax deduction.

At age thirty-four he was honored by being made a trustee of the prestigious California Science Institute. At the second trustees' board meeting he attended, one agenda item was how to raise the funds for a new center for study of advancing technology's impact on society (which, in the first meeting, he had convinced the board of trustees they should create). He told them that he had a wealthy foreign friend who might provide the money, one who he knew would insist on being anonymous. The funds soon arrived in the form of a transfer from a Swiss bank to the university's bank. Although he had said nothing to suggest or encourage it, the other trustees concocted the theory that it was Robert Curtis who had provided those funds but had chosen to keep the philanthropy secret. So they surprised him by publicly announcing that the new building would be named "The Robert Curtis Center."

Trustees of the California Science Institute, the Governor of California, and certain other appropriate individuals of prominence were later assembled in a luncheon to celebrate the opening of the Center's beautiful new Robert Curtis Center. The speeches were highly complementary about Robert Curtis who found himself seated next to none other than Allen Hamilton, now retired from Palotek and also a Trustee of the Institute.

The two talked about old times at Palotek, Hamilton especially commenting on how important Robert's contributions had been to the company's success both before and after he had left it. Then, when lunch was over, Hamilton asked Robert if he could take the time to join him for a short walk, saying he had something he wished to say privately.

"I've been wanting to get something off my mind, Robert, actually for years," he said. "I was always waiting for the right time, but it seemed never to arrive. Maybe today is that right time, after you've been honored for what you are and what you've accomplished. I'm sure that the anonymous donor of the new Center must be Schaeffer and Bonner and I know that they became you. You see, I used to see a list of payments made to all subcontractors of Palotek that exceeded $100,000 per year."

Shocked by these last words, Robert turned immediately to face Hamilton but Hamilton continued to look straight ahead as they walked. What did he mean? What was he saying? Of course, Robert thought, my company is the former Schaeffer and Bonner, which became Curtis,

Schaeffer and Bonner when I joined it. Was Hamilton telling me, by mentioning the $100,000, that he had discovered my scheme, or that he had known all along? I always knew he saw the invoices, of course. But how much did he know? What was he going to say next?

"You're greatly admired by everyone, Robert, especially me and you know it," continued Hamilton. "So I doubt you will choose to take offense at what I'm going to tell you."

"Here it comes," thought Robert, growing more fearful.

"You were not treated right at Palotek, Robert, and that was my doing. Let me tell you why it's important for me to admit that. It's really — to get right to it — because I'm so ashamed of it. You were so much smarter than the rest of us that I should have made you the heir apparent of the company's leadership. After a little time as my principal assistant, I should have appointed you president and then you would have taken over as chairman and chief executive from me after I retired. What a CEO of Palotek you would have been! What you could have done with that company! But I didn't give you that chance."

"Why didn't you, Allen? I guess that's what you want to tell me," Robert replied, not yet fully relieved. He was still wondering whether Hamilton was going to return to Schaeffer and Bonner.

"Look, Robert, I was far from ready to retire then. I knew if I made you my assistant, and then the president, I would quickly become excess baggage. You wouldn't have needed me. You could have made all the necessary decisions for the company without putting up with the nuisance of having to discuss things with the chairman. Actually, I really couldn't share control with someone so brilliant, so much smarter. That is, forgive me, what I'm ashamed of."

"Allen," Robert said, "I don't believe this. First of all, I don't accept that you would have lacked confidence in your own competence, as you are implying so strongly. Besides, bringing me into the top corporate office to share overall responsibility with you when I was so young and had never run an operation — at the least you would have been busy for a long time just teaching me the ropes."

"No, Robert, your breaking-in period would have been damned brief. Hell, Robert, with your brains you could have been extraordinary at any role in the business at any age if only you were given the assignment. I simply wasn't man enough — I didn't choose to so assign you."

"I'm still not convinced you were afraid of me, Allen," Robert replied. "Anyway, you would have done what was best for the company. There had to be another reason why you didn't set out to groom me for president. What was it?"

"Yes, Robert," Allen said, after some hesitation. "And I'm particularly ashamed regarding that other reason. It's very simple — but it's embarrassing to come right out and say it. Damn it, Robert, you were too doggone short and fat. The others made jokes about it constantly. Even as they followed your recommendations and saw their own interests benefiting from your intellect and talent, they used to compete to make cracks about your size and shape. They would curb the comments in my presence after I spoke out a few times. But if I'd made you president, I would have put you in an intolerable situation because they would have disliked enormously reporting to you as their boss. Some of the best would have quit. I was convinced it wouldn't work.

"Well — I was wrong. I went along with the prejudice. Maybe that means I was the most prejudiced of all. What do you think, Robert? Could you have bossed those guys

— even as they looked down at you — with your knowing they were not accepting you as their leader?"

"I think so," Robert said. "Yes, Allen. Sure — they would have given me trouble at first, but that would have stopped after I established my intellectual and innovative strengths at every encounter. I would have gotten them to look up to me despite my being physically low."

"You really think that, Robert?"

"Yes — well — not totally, Allen. Making me president — you can be forgiven for not taking that enormous risk. What I went and did with my career was a sure thing — not a gamble. Maybe short and fat geniuses should start their own companies, as I did — be their own bosses. So — you don't have to be ashamed about not making me president, Allen. But, still, you know what? Maybe you should have tried it. Maybe you should have ignored the prejudice and thus fought it."

"Yes, Robert, I should have. By not having the guts to go ahead and do it, I came up short as a chief executive."

"Not short maybe, but then you weren't ten feet tall either, Allen" Robert replied with a big grin that made apparent his satisfaction with that reply.

They walked along silently, comfortable in each other's company, as they approached their parked cars.

Did Allen Hamilton know about the fraud? If he did, Robert thought to himself, maybe Hamilton wanted his silence to be a sort of compensation to me for his failure to give me my deserved place in the company. Since I was both the victim of that prejudice, thus deserving compensation, and also the perpetrator of a fraud resulting from it, from which I benefited, did the two negatives counter each other? Did that even things up? No, I don't think so, Robert had to confess, if only to himself.

Before parting from his old boss, Robert felt he wanted to say something more to Hamilton — a necessary minimum.

"You took the easy path, Allen," said Robert. "But considering everything, that's not something you should be terribly apologetic about. I want you to know that I took the easy path too, once in the past when I had a big problem to handle. I'm also ashamed of how I handled it. What I did wasn't right. I've agonized about it ever since, for years, with more cause, I think, than you should feel about your action, Allen."

"Well — Robert," Alan replied. "You weren't ten feet tall either."

Chapter 5: The Stockholder's Gazette

"What a marvelous location for a house — high up on these rocks. The ocean waves are breaking right under this balcony! How long have you lived here, Mr. Dillingham?"

"I bought this land two years ago, right after I sold my stock in the Gazette for over twenty million dollars. Whoops! You haven't turned that tape recorder on yet, have you? I hate people who talk about their money and I just did. This property originally had just a little guesthouse on it with its own bit of private beach. It was split off from the big estate next door when some old movie mogul who owned it all died. I paid under a half million and I knocked that nothing structure down. I've just moved into this new home that cost me two million to build. I was offered six million for the property last month. And don't for hell sakes call me Mr. Dillingham, because I'm going to call you Scotty, certainly not Mr. Coleson, and next week I'll turn twenty-seven, which I'll bet is less years than you've done interviews."

"OK. I'm Scotty, you're Greg. And you guessed right. I've done interviews for a bit over thirty years. There, now my recorder is plugged in, or do you want to move inside? I'd prefer to sit out here and watch the waves while we talk if you don't mind. Greg."

"You've come all the way from New York to talk to me, Scotty, so, hell, you can sit wherever you want. Won't the surf's breakers bother that recorder? No? I can just talk at this conversational level? Good. Alright, now that I'm on the public record, I'll be more careful. But first, just one more indiscretion. How old are you, Scotty? I don't really give a damn, you understand, but if you've been at this for thirty years, you've got to be into your fifties and —"

"And, from the comments you've been quoted as making, Greg, anybody over twenty-nine is old to you. So I, at fifty-seven — you must be wondering if I will make it through this interview."

"Not really. But I'm the youngest business entrepreneur you've ever interviewed. True? So, let's get going, Scotty, old boy."

"Yes, let's. I'm going to ask lots of questions, Greg. But I won't keep pressing you on anything you don't really want to discuss. I hope we can just talk and let the conversation go where it will. Of course, even though it's all been written about plenty, I will certainly want to hear straight from you how you happened to get the idea for the Stockholder's Gazette in the first place. How in the world you conceived the totally radical, unprecedented scheme of creating a huge subscription and stockholders base on the Internet before even one single issue had ever appeared. How by now you see your unusual actions — I mean like your suddenly selling the Gazette so early. And, again, even though you may think you've answered that question enough times, I've got to ask you directly about what went wrong. Why the Gazette is in bankruptcy in its fourth year, so soon after being such a huge stock market sensation."

"Alright, Scotty. Here it is. First, the invention of the Gazette. It was a direct result of a speech to employees that old man Oliver delivered. I'd worked for Oliver publications less than a year. Of course, I'd never met the man. What that relic had to say was a shocker to me. Most importantly—"

"Old man Oliver? That relic, you called him. Come on now, Greg. Andy Oliver was written up recently as planning to retire when he hits sixty-five next year. So he was only early sixties when you heard that speech. You notice I'm smiling as I put this next question to you, because you've been written up as immature, a smart-aleck — no respect for your elders. Would you care to add anything more about the doddering Oliver?"

"Yes, I would. The great Andrew Wells Oliver, the publishing icon — he is not the Oliver of decades ago. The young Oliver started seven successful magazines, seven, and he bought and built up four more, and he got himself a net worth of nearly a hundred million bucks before he was forty. He owned a leading weekly in every field he entered. Amazing! A top magazine in business, sports, travel, home decorating, even fashion! He put together a hot management team for each publication. But, hell, that was over a quarter of a century ago. He hasn't done a damn thing for twenty-five years. Hasn't changed his teams. Except for one death, each of the seven sheets are still in the hands of his original guys, only instead of their being twenty-five to thirty-five, they're now fifty to sixty years old. None of them has had an idea for a decade — hell, longer than that."

"But Greg, Oliver did hire you, and other fresh college graduates."

"Yes, but I modestly suggest that hardly makes up for the negatives of Oliver's aging cast. When people get old they stop creating. Look, I know that, sure, people can get wiser with experience. So as they age they should become advisors. They should quit being managing executives. Because they've made lots of mistakes and they've seen more, they can help you avoid mistakes. They can help you handle routine management complexities because they've done it a lot before. But aging screws up every talent known to man. Take scientists — Einstein — they say his was the most creative mind in science in centuries — but all his great discoveries were made when he was young. He kept trying and trying after he passed forty, after the avalanche of his brilliant breakthroughs was over. He couldn't come through with a single great additional idea. Nobel awardees —virtually all made their big discoveries when they were young. Of course, the worst indictment on Oliver -- proof that he is far past his prime — is what happened to the Stockholder's Gazette when he bought the controlling shares from me."

"Before we get into that, Greg, tell me, what exactly was it in Oliver's speech that got you so riled up that you invented the Gazette?"

"He told us it was dumb to start a new magazine."

"Maybe, Greg, that was why he quit starting new ones," said Scotty. "He decided he had some wonderful cash cows and that, in contrast, new magazines were unlikely to make money. Maybe too much competition now from the Internet. Maybe he was right, Greg, that starting new magazines was no longer sensible. But even if he was wrong, why did his views inspire you?

"Look, Scotty, here was a guy I had naively assumed — me with my useless master's degree in English literature — that he should be my role model. I was going to emulate him. I wanted to start new publications, grow them to big circulations -- educate, inform, entertain. The world sure as hell needs new publications. I was all excited to start them. All kinds of important subjects are uncovered. New magazines, if they're good, should make money. Probably less and less by printing on paper, but on the Internet. So, I was plotting to find a way to get in to see Oliver. I was sure I could sell him on the idea that there was an opening for a weekly publication designed especially for people that play the stock market hoping to beat the system. I'm talking about the tens of millions of small, individual investors, not the professionals, not those who have a billion and depend on professionals to manage their investments for them. I wanted to reach the huge bunch of speculators, guys who look at the market quotations every day and try to pick stocks that will go up. They're gamblers really, not investors. They want to beat the odds the same as the guys that play the horses or bet on football games or go to Las Vegas. I thought I knew this throng of bettors would buy a magazine really put together for them just right."

"Why, Greg, didn't you just tell your immediate boss about your idea and ask him to help you get to the right executive — someone assigned to planning for expansion of the company?"

"My boss? You have to be kidding, Scotty. Marty Gibson was in charge of final editing on one of the seven magazines and I was one of his flunkies, the junior one. He had me scanning articles about to be published to catch typos. That zombie fuddy-duddy Gibson wouldn't have known what to make of my idea. He had no business sense. It wasn't his job to have any. He wouldn't have known where to send me even if he liked the idea. First of all, there was no so-called planning department in the company. Hell, old man Oliver was it. Eleven managers of eleven magazines reported to Oliver — as did the book company's president, of course. Mind you, the company's revenues were around two hundred million a year and yet each piece of the operation was headed by a manager who was an antique — a dodo with no imagination, no zeal for building the company. The big, play-it-safe overall manager, Oliver, a worn out has-been — he was the company's sole business strategist."

"What reasons did he give in his talk for not starting any new magazines, Greg?"

"He had lots of reasons, Scotty. The big ones were the huge start-up cost and the big risk of failure — both really old stuff. Even I had heard it ten times. Before you can sell advertising you have to have a large subscription list. But that takes years even with the most attractive magazine content imaginable, he lectured. All that time you're spending money on promotion, text, staff, marketing, printing, mailing, and so on."

"But, Greg, as you said — that's old stuff — just plain fact. Starting a new magazine means high risk, a long period of start-up investment. Why did his saying that shock you and cause you to invent the fantastic combination you created with the Gazette — the ingenious new way to get the capital through the Internet, the unique mission you concocted for the paper, the big list of committed subscribers?"

"Aw — but Scotty — don't you see? Without knowing it, that fossil, Oliver, was spelling it out for me. You can't get money from investors to start a magazine if you aren't already selling ads, lots of ads. But you can't sell ads without a lot of subscribers. So! Voila! The first subscribers should be the investors! Remember this is to be a paper for stock buying gamblers."

"Greg, wait a minute! How could you have thought you could get a lot of people to subscribe to a magazine that doesn't exist, that is put out by a corporation that also doesn't exist and won't even be founded unless the subscribers subscribe? How? I know you did it, but how did you come to imagine that you could?"

"Well, Scotty, you have to have a real feel for those guys who gamble on the stock market. Then, you would know they would be crazy about being in at the very start of a company with a clearly new idea. They'll buy the stock and at the same time subscribe to the magazine, because this particular gamble couples the stock sale and the subscriptions. They will figure the stock they bought will go up every time more stock is bought because with every stock sale the subscriber list also goes up. Now, what do you put in the magazine so they'll all want to read it? Again, remember the audience. That leads you to what the editorial content should be. Should I go on, Scotty? You know what happened."

"Yes, Greg. I know you succeeded in getting the Gazette launched and funded because over 100,000 — more like 200,000 — individuals actually did subscribe and bought a stock share after they read your proposal on the Internet. But I don't understand some subtleties about the scheme. You make it seem so easy. If you'd come to me with the idea originally, I surely would have told you that you can't sell a subscription for two years for fifty dollars and a share of common stock for another fifty dollars to 100,000 individuals without a national network of agents whom you couldn't persuade to organize to do it. A piddling one hundred bucks for each single transaction? Really! For God's sake, the marketing cost alone, the months of intensive advertising, promoting, and selling — all that required activity would consume funds dwarfing the money you could hope to raise, I would have argued. Besides, the Securities and Exchange Commission wouldn't have let you do the selling.

"Scotty, I ignored the SEC."

"What do you mean you ignored the SEC? Nobody sells stock to the public and ignores the S.E.C., not even a brash, young genius. I know you solicited stock sales mainly on the world-wide Web and your single full page Wall Street Journal ad was loaded with fine print. I assume you submitted the ads for approval to the S.E.C. ahead of time. You did, didn't you?"

"Nope. Not until I had the checks in from over 100,000 subscribers and company share-buyers did I go to the S.E.C. Look -- I promised in the ads to found the company only if I received the money for 100,000 shares from 100,000 separate subscribers and that only then would I apply for S.E.C. approval."

"I don't get how your ads got by the S.E.C."

"As the ads said, all checks were to be made out to Bailey, Frank and Henderson, you know, B.F.&H., the big public accounting firm. If less than 100,000 checks were received, I said they would all be torn up. If enough came in, only then would I take the legal steps required to create the new corporation and the new weekly."

"Of course, I read that you did that. This is the first time I've heard of the starting and financing of a new company on the Internet. I mean you sold individual shares — in the hundreds of thousands — on the Internet. That's really original. You couldn't have done that kind of sale through the usual stock-selling routes. If you didn't get the company started all you had to do was to throw out the checks, never cash them. You really did by-pass the SEC. I see that. That's another first. That's all pretty darn impressive. You really broke new ground.

"You personally took the whole financial risk, Greg. I remember reading that too. You gave yourself a third of the stock in the new company as a reward for your novel idea, your deserved promoting and organizing, and for your risk taking. How much would you have lost if you got too few takers but still had to pay for the ads and the rest?"

"All of it, Scotty. My entire net worth. I paid for all the initial expenses out of my own pocket. It was around 250,000 dollars. Of course, B.F.&H — I made a deal with them. They did all the administrative stuff with the stock buyers and didn't charge me. I gave them a block of stock, you see, which they sold a bit later. They did well."

"You were twenty-three. Where'd you get 250,000 dollars? Inherited it? Saved it from your big salary at Oliver?"

"I made it in the stock market."

"You started playing the market — what, at age twenty-one?"

"No — age thirteen."

"You bought and sold shares at thirteen?"

"The stock was in my dad's name as guardian-custodian until I reached twenty-one. Look, Pop ran the only brokerage office in Pocatello, Idaho where I was born. All I heard at home as a kid was stock market talk. At eleven I was picking stocks. I was captivated by the market. Pop and his friends got a big kick out of it. I would read all the reports he brought home, the so-called analyses that the brokers feed their clients. He gave me a pretend two hundred dollars and I quickly worked it up to seven hundred, mostly by guessing right on the new issues, the new small companies. A large fraction of these start-up companies were presented more optimistically than sounded real to me. Scotty, I knew instinctively that those stocks were being over-hyped. I would buy some shares when they were first issued, wait for the market's first wave of overbidding, and then sell to get the really undeserved quick gain before everybody wised up and the price dropped. Scotty, I'm still doing it. Anybody — you — you can still do it now. I've just given you a freebee, my tested secret. A typical new public issue is announced at around twenty dollars a share. Some don't sell well. Some, however, attract too many buyers and the price rises to thirty or forty in a hurry. Then, just a little later, it naturally goes back down. I think it's easy to pick these flash in the pan high riders. Something about what they're up to or how they are described attracts the gamblers."

"But this was all a game when you were a kid — that two hundred dollars wasn't real money."

"Until I was thirteen. Then my dad gave me an even thousand actual bucks for my birthday and told me he'd place the orders for me on stock choices I gave him. He even let me buy on margin but he also made very clear that if I couldn't cover a loss, he'd never give me more and I'd be broke. I think he figured I'd soon lose the thousand, and learn not to gamble in the market."

"Instead you made yourself a few hundred thousand! But, coming back to the Gazette, Greg, why didn't your attorney tell you not to place the ads in the Web or the Wall Street Journal because of possible later civil suits?"

"What attorney? I didn't have any attorney. What could people sue me about? My Internet ads clearly stated that if the company was never formed, I would do what I promised — tear up the checks."

"You got so much free publicity, Greg. I know the Wall Street Journal said that a hundred times more was said about your new venture -- in all the business magazines and daily newspapers and on TV and the Internet -- than was reported about any new company in all stock market history. "

"Yes, Scotty. After my very first ad, the stories started. First it was about my gall in expecting people to buy my pig in a poke. Then it shifted to daily reporting of the latest total of buyers — 10,000, 20,000, 50,000, 100,000. When I was interviewed on TV by Jay Leno the number of shareholder-subscribers that evening was already past 80,000. Everyone wanted to gamble one hundred dollars and be in on the fun. All the publicity I got would have cost millions if I had had to pay for it."

"It overshot didn't it?"

"You mean I went past the 100,000 subscribers and shareholders? Yes, I decided to stop selling at 200,000. That gave me 20 million dollars, more than enough to print and send out all the copies we were committed to for two years and, of course, hiring a good staff."

"But, Greg, weren't you worried about the Gazette touting stocks, or being accused of it."

"Oh, no. I planned from the beginning — even included it in my ads on the Web — that neither I nor any member of the Gazette's staff would ever write an article mentioning any specific stock or even any category of stocks — like computer companies, say. Of course, my outside authors were free to write what they wanted. Moreover, each issue of the Gazette contained, on every page in large letters, that the reader should be aware that all authors might have an ax to grind, might be pushing stocks they own, or trying to drive down the prices of stocks they plan to buy."

"Actually, even after you had sold those 200,000 shares, more subscribers came aboard, didn't they?"

"Yes — over 100,000 just plain subscriptions were bought, on the Internet, with no stock, before they had ever seen a first issue. Even I didn't expect that. Of course, some were buying the stock of the original shareholders."

"The stock price more than doubled before the first issue of the paper hit the stands, did it not?"

"More than quadrupled. Many shareholders — remember they had bought only one lousy share for fifty dollars — sold it for two hundred or more using our Internet Website. Big deal! They netted a hundred dollar capital gain or so, some at the top of the trading, a thousand. Trivial! The gamblers, you see, couldn't resist doing it. It was sort of an ego thing, something to brag to friends about."

"And that by itself, that funny, big trading by individuals on the Internet and the phenomenal bidding up of the shares -- that gave you more publicity."

"Yep! The Wall Street Journal, the New York Times Business Section, the L.A. Times, papers everywhere — they all reported daily the price of sales on the Internet.

"Everybody wanted to own a share. Of course, some guys wanted to own lots of shares. Some would get up to ten or twenty shares and unload at an insane price to others who were determined to own hundreds or thousands. All the speculators were after holding the record. One guy — I forget his name — was said to have had the championship at one point with over 2000 shares."

"So, you were excited. Tell me how you felt about all this — at age twenty-three causing this barrage of precedents, publicity, personal fame, and challenge? Then there was your problem — I guess it was a tremendous problem — of publishing that first issue."

"My God, was it a problem! But not the way you're thinking. The problem wasn't planning what would be in that issue. The planning of it was taken away from me."

"What do you mean?"

"I mean, Scotty, that several big name economists, an ex-secretary of the treasury, no less than four CEOs of big investment banks, a gang of business columnists, numerous professors, all kinds of celebrities in the world of finance — they all wanted to author an article in this first edition, this paper that the whole stock market world was awaiting. They were calling — hell, it was impossible for me to use my office phone. They begged me. It was huge pressure. It became clear that I should print up an extra million copies of the first issue to be sold at the newsstands, far beyond the subscription list. Scalpers made me fantastic offers to buy 1,000 copies or 10,000 copies if I would get those copies to them ahead of the general circulation. Clearly that was going to be the journal's mission — printing articles about the stock market by big names."

"That first issue, Greg — I know it went down in history as the publication with the most remarkable assembly of pieces about the stock market ever put out — the market's characteristics, what makes it tick, where it is headed."

"And don't forget, Scotty, I published it soon after as a little book — sold over two million paper-back copies of the book. It was quickly translated into seven languages — French, German, Italian, Spanish, Portuguese in Brazil, Japanese, and even Russian. The foreign rights brought in a nice extra profit."

"Alright then, I think it's time, Greg, to get to what went wrong. Why did you sell your shares and divorce yourself from the Gazette so soon? What? Eleven months?"

"Ten months, Scotty. First, look, I'm basically a stock market gambler. I could see that the Gazette's stock price had gotten up way too high, so how could I not sell? And how could I stay on as the Chief Executive of the paper if I sold all my stock? Besides, look who wanted my shares — Andrew Oliver!"

"And he offered you a high price — right?"

"I thought crazy high! I would not have sold at that price to anyone else because I knew it was too high. But my overcharging old Oliver? That was irresistible! Besides I knew the period ahead was going to be tough. The magazine was going to fade out in its popularity unless a lot of work was done. It was not going to be fun for me to attempt it."

"But, everything had been going well, hadn't it?"

"No, Scotty. I knew the test was going to be to get the subscribers to renew their subscriptions for after the two prepaid years. I offered inducements for early re-subscribing. It flopped. New subscriptions and renewals -- nothing.

"Why?"

"Well, at first every shareholder naturally pressed all his friends to subscribe. After all, more subscriptions meant more advertising revenue and more profits and hence a higher value for their stock. But, let me tell you, all those articles written by all those big names? They were boring — really boring. I quickly gave up reading the articles. I figured the subscribers — they couldn't be reading the Gazette either. The stupid advertisers looked only at the fact that we had that big number of subscribers."

"Wait a minute, Greg, what you're telling me means — well — that you really didn't have the mission of the Gazette right. You really took advantage of Oliver."

"What? Me? Age twenty-four, going on twenty-five? I understood something that Oliver was missing? With all his decades of experience are you saying he didn't—maybe couldn't—size up properly the property he was buying and so he paid too much for my stock?"

"He did just that, didn't he Greg? Anyway, you are out and rich. The Gazette indeed did lose its readers and the advertising revenue had to start down."

"That's a colossal understatement, Scotty. Almost no one renewed. It was a catastrophe."

"But that was over a year ago. It was only two weeks ago that the Gazette declared bankruptcy. That's why I'm interviewing you now. What was Oliver doing all this last year? And I trust you also noticed that Oliver was right — I mean, he said don't start new magazines."

"He had one of his old cronies in charge and he did the usual things. You know, if you need more subscriptions, you drop the price — you add prizes. With each subscription, you offer Oliver's books for bonuses — then —"

"Greg, didn't I see issues of the Gazette," interrupted Scotty, "during the entire last year, and they still had lots of ads?"

"Yes. Oliver practically gave the advertisers the space free. All that time he kept publishing the same kind of articles, those that this group of stock market gamblers were not reading."

"Why didn't Oliver change the content or shut the Gazette down — say, a year earlier — when the subscriptions didn't get renewed and there was all the evidence he needed that it was not going to be a money maker — especially if he had no ideas on how to change the paper so it would attract readers. Why didn't he liquidate the corporation and send the remaining funds to the stockholders? Why go on until the company was broke and even owed money for rent and some pay to employees and fees to authors?"

"Because Oliver was cheap — yes, cheap is the correct word. But I'm not complaining. The bankruptcy was good for me because I wanted to buy the paper back."

"Greg, did you think to make an offer to Oliver to repurchase your big block of stock? Had he sold off some shares in the interim?"

"The bankruptcy meant I didn't have to deal with Oliver at all. I didn't have to buy Oliver's or anybody else's stock. I dealt with the bankruptcy trustee appointed by the court. I offered to buy the Gazette, pay off all outstanding debts, pay for the desks, paper, pencils and all other assets, at book value, plus one dollar for the 'good-will.' The trustee was delighted. The formalities will be complete next week. I'll own the Gazette and I'll start it up again."

"Really! Are you going to sell a share of stock with each subscription again? Have you got the Internet ads ready for the market gamblers?"

"Yes, Scotty. How did you guess?"

"Come on now! You're not serious! I was joking when I asked. I'm going to say it, Greg. Who the hell is going to buy the shares this time, after the Gazette has gone bankrupt and its subscribers haven't renewed and the original subscribers don't want to read the damn articles."

"Because I've got a great new idea, Scotty. Besides the Gazette wasn't a failure while I was in charge. It went bust when a passé guy took over. I have the original list of investors. They're all still playing the market. They've all been on a fascinating adventure with me. They've been players in an exciting, first time ever game, all on account of me personally. They'll sign up for my next trip because of my new plan. Also, this time I'm going to promise to stay with it for a long time."

"Until you get old — like maybe forty?"

"I was thinking more like thirty-five. Anyway, Scotty do you want me to put you down for a package? That's a year's subscription for fifty dollars and one share of common for fifty dollars for a total of one hundred dollars."

"No! Definitely, no, Greg! Not until you tell me what the new Gazette is going to be. What is this great new idea of yours? What will I find in the Gazette that will hold my interest, every issue, every week?"

"I'm not going to tell you the new idea. You'll read about it on the Internet in six weeks. What I'm planning for the text of the Gazette has never been done before. You'll be impressed. And this time, I'll sell no more than 50,000 shares. I plan to attract another 50,000 subscribers soon after without any share purchases added. With 100,000 paid subscribers, I'll be able to roll. So, you see if you don't commit to me now, you may not be able to get hold of a share; they'll go fast. It'll be necessary to sign up early to become a shareholder. The shareholders will have some interesting privileges."

"What privileges?"

"It will be fully described in my announcement. So, how about it? Will you risk a lousy hundred dollars. What do you say? Are you in?"

"Nope. Well — one hundred bucks, huh? What the hell. Put me down, Greg."

"Good."

"Do you want this hundred-dollar bill now, Greg?"

"No, no. When the announcement and solicitation comes out you send a check."

"O.K. But because I have committed early, ahead of your public campaign, you have to tell me right now your idea for the new Gazette's content. I'll keep the secret — tell no one."

"No, Scotty, I can't do that"

"Of course you can, Greg."

"I shouldn't. But, all right. I'll gamble that you'll not tell. All articles in the Gazette will be by the stock-holders themselves — the subscribers, the market gamblers. They'll all be short write-ups. These guys are full of ideas about the market, the stocks to buy, what the government regulators should do and not do, what's wrong with CEOs and corporate board directors. I know these gambler characters. They'll love to see their names in print and knowing that only the subscribers, the members of the "club," will have their thoughts published. I'll energize them with questions to comment on. We'll be swamped with responses. We'll publish only the good ones. Everyone whose piece is accepted will get a free subscription for the following year."

"But Greg, they'll just push various stocks they own to get the prices up or pan stocks they plan to buy to get the price down."

"Of course they might. Why not? Free speech in our country you know. We'll always remind the readers that the Gazette is not responsible for and does not influence or back up what the writer-subscribers say."

"Well, Greg, I must say that it's now a most peculiar and novel trio — the stockholders, the subscribers, the authors — they will be all one and the same group of people."

"It will work, Scotty. Gamblers like to talk with gamblers. They'll talk to each other in the new Gazette, and, of course, we'll also put the talk on the Internet in the right way — you know, to make the most money. Want to bet on it? Whether it will be a success this time?"

"No, Greg. I'll just watch and I'll write about it, whether it works or not. Either result is going to be fascinating, I'm sure, for my readers."

Chapter 6: President and Chief Jesting Officer

I'm not here, doctor, because I can't sleep. I'm not having headaches. And I'm not looking to come here weekly and be psychoanalyzed for a year.

What made you ask for an appointment?

I thought you might be able to help me with a bothersome problem I have. It's about my sense of humor.

You're afraid you lack a sense of humor?

No, no, the opposite. I may have an exaggerated sense of humor.

Why do you think that?

Well — it's that I see funny angles about absolutely everything. And I am maybe too prone to bring up those funny angles to others when they are being the most serious. Sometimes I do it when I think others regard some situation as far more serious and important than I think it really is.

Can you give me an example of your exaggerated sense of humor?

Yes — actually something happened on my way up here just a few minutes ago. It's probably typical of the way I overdo. In the lobby I noticed a friend and stopped to say hello. He had someone with him. He said, "Casey, I'd like you to meet Mr. Marx." So right away I came up with, "Which Marx would you be? Harpo, Chico, Groucho, Karl, Toe the, Any Distinguishing, On-Your?"

How did they react?

They laughed. But I shouldn't have done it. Because Mr. Marx laughed doesn't mean he was pleased. He's probably had too many Marx brothers' jokes thrown at him — like: "I've heard of your brothers." I guess my friend, knowing me, was not too surprised.

Do you like making people laugh?

That isn't why I do it. I don't think it's the main reason.

Then why else do you indulge in all that comedy?

Because I communicate better if I do it. I can make points quicker if I employ a humorous twist — on serious subjects.

When you were young, a child, a teenager, in college, were you known as a wit?

You're asking have I always been this way. Always. It's in my genes. My father was Irish, Casey O'Connell. My mother was Jewish, Alexandra Baum. They met because their parents — my two pairs of grandparents — were all in show business -- vaudeville, that is. The Irish pair and the Jewish pair — they were often on the same bill. When my mother and father were first married, in their early twenties, they were a team doing comedy routines. Wrote their own material. They were good, I always understood. They might have become big — who knows. But when vaudeville slumped they started to sell real estate, did extremely well, liked it, stayed in that business together and gradually accumulated a small fortune. They both were funny even as they were dying.

Is that why you have those two middle initials?

You guessed it. My full legal name is Brian C.A. O'Connell. The C and A come from Casey and Alex, the name of my parents' nightclub act.

What about the rest of your family — siblings, children? Are they funny?

I have one brother and one sister. They're funny. I have one son. He's an engineer like me. Only, while I'm aerospace he's computers. Started his own company — with my help, of course. He's not in the least funny. But then, he's a Ph.D. Few engineers and no Ph.D.'s of any kind are funny. He has a little girl, my only grandchild. She's funny. She's the world's only six-year-old stand-up comic. She thinks up things to say, saves them, and comes in when I visit and stands there and rattles them off with perfect timing and a straight face. She knows I want to make her laugh, and so she wants to make me laugh. I guess I've ruined her.

But you really enjoy making her laugh, don't you?

Yes — sure I do — very much.

What's wrong with that?

I'm not aware that there's anything wrong with it. I'm glad I'm witty.

But you have doubts about your being — what — too actively witty?

As the president and chief operating officer, and I think a very successful one, of a large corporation — about to become the chairman and chief executive, when the present chairman retires in less than a year — I am very serious. But I can judge when the situation calls for a light touch, when a little humor can get everyone to ease up. I never take myself too seriously. Half of my humor is at my own expense. Employees should have a good laugh every day at the boss's expense.

So why are you suddenly concerned about this?

Oh, hell — it's my boss, Jim Swanson, our chairman. He brought it up last week. Now, mind you, I've always known that he has no sense of humor. He doesn't laugh when everybody else does. I don't mean just at my own attempts at being funny. When anyone at all tosses off amusing comments, he takes on a forced smile. He doesn't dig why others are laughing.

How long have you been president?

Eight years. Swanson's been chairman over twenty years. He started the company. And yes, he picked me, if that's what you're getting at. He knew me well, comedy and all, and he made me president anyway. He had two presidents before me. He fired the first and the second quit on his own. Swanson got the reputation of being hard on his presidents — hard to get along with. But I've gotten along with Jim Swanson just fine.

What exactly did he do the other day? What disturbed you about it?

Hell — I asked for it by what I did. Jim likes to drop into my office when he has an issue on his mind. He stops by and asks my secretary if I'm alone. If I am, he pokes his head in and asks do I have a few minutes. Then he asks her for a cup of decaf, comes in, sits, very relaxed, and then he gets to his subject. Well, he did just that the other day. He asked me, as he always does, "What's new?" I responded by first telling him I had a dream the night before.

Tell me about the dream.

I guess you mean tell you what I told him was the dream. I actually did have a dream, but I doctored it as I related it to him. Anyway, I told him I dreamt I went to Heaven. Jim asked me how I knew it was Heaven and I said I found myself up among pink clouds and there was a character with wings and a white beard sitting at a reception desk. So I asked him, "Is this Heaven?" And he said, "Yes." And I said, "Well, I guess I have died. What do I do next?" He asked my name and told me to pull up a chair. Then, after he punched some buttons on a computer, he said "We've got a problem in your case." The board of directors, he proceeded to inform me, were meeting at that very moment to decide whether they should from now on refuse entry to businessmen. This fellow at the desk was not St. Peter, it turned out, but just a vice president. St. Peter was upstairs somewhere chairing the board. Anyway, I asked what the reason was that they were considering black-balling businessmen. He then tossed off all those trite things that the media here on Earth are always printing. You know. Like business exists just to make profits so they screw the consumers and don't give a damn about preserving the environment. They control the government — at least when the Republicans are in. So I figured this vice president was a Democrat. When I asked he said they were all above politics up there. Then I found out he'd been on that same job for 1300 years. I asked what happened to the guy that had his job 1300 years ago. He said they simply retired him. Now, I thought that was interesting. I asked what happens to somebody in Heaven when he retires. The answer he gave was that if you're up in Heaven and you retire, you go to Hell, just the same as you do on Earth when you retire.

That was the dream you described to the chairman?

"Yes — and you're thinking the punch line, if you can call it that, was not very funny. And, honestly, I thought the same thing. Worse. That you go to Hell when you retire — here I was, finding myself saying that to the chairman who'll soon retire!

What did the chairman say?

Sure enough, he reminded me that he was about to retire. He then suggested that when he retired it might be a good thing for me to retire what he called the comedian inside of me. He said maybe that comedian has finished his life's work.

Wouldn't that remark mean that he was still planning to make you his successor, thus reassuring you?

In a way, yes, because if he really had other plans, that would have been the moment to say it.

But he didn't say that.

No. He didn't.

Then, what worries you? That you've lost the touch? That you really aren't funny anymore?

No, not really. That one recital of a dream is a bad example. No humorist has a 100 percent batting average. Look at Jay Leno, today's No. 1 professional. He has a big staff of top talent preparing his TV broadcast, yet he bombs on one joke in four or five.

Was that really the first time the chairman ever showed dislike of your proclivity toward humor?

No. The evening I first met Jim Swanson I made the mistake of tossing off some puns. He does not appreciate puns. You may remember that years ago America launched the first spacecraft out to the distant planets. It passed Jupiter and Saturn and sent back signals from way out there. To celebrate, NASA held a reception for TRW, the company that built that successful spacecraft and I was invited because my company had supplied a spacecraft component. I spotted Dr. Mettler, the principal space executive at TRW. He was talking to Jim Swanson. I walked up and said, "Well, by <u>Jupiter</u>, if it isn't Dr. Mettler!" Swanson immediately said, "Good God, we've got a punster here." I answered, "Actually that's my first pun since last <u>Saturnday</u>. It's not too good a pun, but I doubt that it <u>Mars</u> my reputation." Swanson then came right out and said he hated puns. "Doesn't everyone" I replied. You know, Doctor, for some reason many people have to pretend to loathe puns — and punsters. Maybe you can provide a professional explanation for that. But from the look on Swanson's face I knew he really did hate them. I remember saying he should have come back at me with "Casey, come down to <u>Earth</u>!" — but that was before I knew he not only could not pun, but he also was devoid of humor. Anyway, Swanson never thought me as in his family, a <u>Sun</u>, or that his humor would <u>Eclipse</u> mine, if you'll forgive two more bad puns. How is <u>your</u> sense of humor doctor? Do psychoanalysts have a sense of humor? Silly question. You must have, to be able to put up with all us nuts who come to you. Maybe you hate puns though.

But he went on to hire you as president of his company?

Yes — a few months after that first meeting. But he didn't make me president because of my sense of humor. He did it despite his not possessing one. My company, which I had founded, was smaller than his. He bought mine for cash. It made me rich. He offered me president of the combine.

The combined company has prospered hasn't it?

True. The company is highly regarded. Jim Swanson has great competence. We're good partners. He's especially good on financial matters. Outstanding actually. I can't think of a single mistake he has ever made as to when to sell common stock, or preferred, or issue bonds, or borrow from banks, or do mergers.

How is he with people?

You're ahead of me. I was just going to say that dealing with people is Swanson's weakness. That's where I've been absolutely necessary to the company. You show me someone who has no sense of humor and I'll show you someone who does not comprehend people. To be witty you've got to understand how and why people think as they do, what bothers them, what pleases them. Look, humor has to do with people and only people. The sun and the moon, the rain or wind or a volcano or bacteria or a nuclear power plant or a spacecraft or a rose or a tree — none of them are funny. People are. If you don't dig how comical people can be, you don't understand people.

But he wouldn't have made you president of the combined company after the merger if he really hated punsters would he?

Well — now that you mention it — there was one time, one pun I pulled off in front of him. I had scored a "four-in-one." In punning, a four-in-one is even a bigger accomplishment for a punster than a hole-in-one is for a golfer. You may recall that a number of years ago there was this best seller book called "Portnoy's Complaint," by Philip Roth. Everybody was reading it. Well, around that time I happened to arrive at a meeting that I was to chair and that Jim Swanson was attending. As everyone was getting into place around the table, two guys were arguing loudly. One of them who lived close to the airport was complaining bitterly that the noise was killing him and that something should be done about the airport noise. And the other guy was telling him that if he couldn't stand the airport noise he ought to move away from the airport. When everyone was finally on hand and seated, and they were still arguing, I banged on the table and said, "<u>We have not gathered here to hear you two air-port-noise-complaints</u>" — a four-in-one. The debaters shut up suddenly and the rest of the group applauded me — except Jim Swanson. The look on his face was one of — well — disgust would be the word. His expression would not have been different if I had thrown up on the table.

Even so, you didn't quit punning? You went on being funny, didn't you?

Correct.

How did you happen to write this book?

How did you get that copy? I saw it sitting here when I came in. I thought you probably dragged it out of your storage bin and placed it there to flatter me — to build up my confidence. "<u>HOW TO PAINT SCENERY BADLY by the World's Worst Artist</u>"

The book was a best seller, wasn't it?

Over 100,000 hard copies. The publisher was amazed. So was I. I got a huge batch of fan mail from amateur artists from everywhere who said that book helped them to avoid botching their paintings. That's what we amateur painters do, you know. We botch paintings. We get a fair start on a painting, get about half-way, and then we do something unintentionally that spoils it. In fact the chapter on just that I titled "Botches and Sons of Botches."

Were you trying to be funny when you thought up that chapter title?

No. Here's the thing — you see — when you commit a botch on a canvas, too often you try to fix it by a series of touch-ups, each of which always makes the painting worse. Those added mars are follow-ons, descendants of the original botch, hence they are properly called "Sons of Botches." It's the right name. It happens accidentally to come out a funny pun that helps make the serious point. A painting can maybe stand a botch and still be good but not several botches each with its own group of sons of botches.

That book on painting caused a stir, I recall. Weren't you accused by some art experts of being too flippant about what artistic talent is all about?

Well — yes. Some art critics were less than complementary about the comments in my book about how artists and critics take themselves too serious. What better proof can you have that I was right than their actually paying so much attention to my urging the readers — presumably amateurs, dilettantes like me, who have fun painting and are not planning any shows — to relax and paint so as to maximize their enjoyment. They should not try always to turn out a product professionals might rate highly.

Do you think of yourself as a Renaissance Man? After all, you are a wealthy industrialist, a successful entrepreneur, a top executive, and also a published author, a skilled painter — and a talented wit? How do you see yourself?

How can I be a Renaissance man? I was too young then to have known Leonardo de Vinci. Shook hands with Leo a couple of times at large parties, but never got to really know him.

Is that answer a demonstration of modesty or an effort to be funny?

What I want is to be thought very serious but good at using humor to express serious thoughts.

If you hear a really funny joke do you remember it and tell it to your friends?

No.

Never?

Never.

But you do sometimes try just being funny?

Well — yes. I do that sometimes.

But you don't want to do it ever. True?

I'd sooner not.

Why not? Why not be funny whenever you feel like it?

To say funny things just to amuse? I don't aspire to be an entertainer.

And, moreover, to be perceived as an entertainer — is it the wrong image for a chairman of the board? You're worried about keeping your funny bone under discipline, aren't you?

True. But I need to be me. I am witty. If I can't be the CEO and still be myself then I don't want to be the CEO.

So what's bothering you?

Nothing.

Nothing?

"Nothing any more. I came in here today with some troubling doubts. I wasn't sure exactly what about. I don't feel that way now. I'm not sure why, but I feel different, better, not worried. I guess this session did it, doctor. I guess I was right in coming to see you. Maybe I'll come again someday, when I have another problem. Unless, of course, you've retired by then and — "

And gone to — ?

Precisely. It would be too funny to seek an appointment with you there.

Chapter 7: Fatal Succession

I did it! I can't believe I did it! Fifteen years I've been the executive secretary to Richard Kirby Reese and never once did I eavesdrop. I don't mean when RK would ask me to stay on the line and make notes. Sure, plenty of times I was very curious about a phone call, when I knew big things were going to be discussed. But for me to listen in was unthinkable. This time — when the doctor from Mayo called — I had to know what he was going to say because I had gotten myself into a panic over RK's health. First those hospital visits here, and then he had me set up his trip to Mayo. The hush-hush tone he used when he directed me to make the arrangement. But especially, RK was not looking right for weeks. Oh, he's looked tired plenty of times. Why not? He's seventy-five and still in charge of everything. Sees few people in his office. Just phones and gives people precise orders. Has all the data on his computer from all over the company and has his finger on everything going on. Often bypasses his so-called president and his vice presidents. Doesn't really believe in delegation even though the company passed two billion dollars sales last year. I decided months ago that this time he's not just tired. He's sick. Even at seventy-five he's still dapper and handsome and full of verve and excitement. I mean he was. Now I know. Inoperable brain tumor, the doctor said. Less than a year. My God!

*   *   *   *   *

Why didn't I fall apart completely when I first heard? And what am I now mainly upset about? Is it really RK? I'm worrying a lot about him, no question. What he's feeling? How will he handle it? It's two days that RK has known, and I'm now listening in on every call, except if another call suddenly comes in or someone walks into my office. I'm getting good at shifting quickly and covering up. Can I help him? RK's wife died years ago, before my time. None of the few women he's been with since I've been his secretary are active with him now. He has his son, of course. But he hasn't talked to him about it. Junior hasn't phoned and RK hasn't phoned him since the Mayo call. He doesn't even see his son except at the company. That's the kind of relationship they have. He has old Underwood who takes care of his home. A cold fish. RK has certainly told Underwood nothing. And Underwood — not until the final day will he see any change in RK. Sure, I'm worried about RK. I'm not in love with him anymore. Not that I ever was. But for a while maybe I thought I was. Off and on. Actually, that's not true, completely. What really happened was that he spoiled other men for me. When I was chosen for the job I was not quite thirty and he was almost sixty for God's sake. But he didn't look it. He was dashing. When I first came to work in the company, when I was only twenty four, it was after my divorce. I was very fussy then about men, naturally. No second mistake for me, and no one who would not be a good father for little Jenny. Which ruled out a lot of possibilities right away and I didn't much care. But in a couple of years I became interested, really interested, in finding the right man. And I had a series of possibilities interested in me. My figure was great. It's still pretty darn good today, for a thirty-eight year old. When I moved up to be RK's secretary all the men I met suddenly seemed lacking. Maybe I came to love RK but I was never <u>in love</u> with him. I have a feeling of almost overwhelming sadness when I think of what he will go through in the next few months! Honest truth is I'm also horrified about what will happen to me. Who will take over running the company? Chances are whoever it is will want his own secretary, not RK's. I'll be offered a job somewhere in the company. But I couldn't handle the comedown. After being the company's number one secretary for so long I can't drop down to a lower office. I'll have to leave. I look in the late twenties. Well, maybe I do. And I'm good at my job. But I've got to be realistic. There aren't that many chief executive officers' secretary jobs out there. CEOs of big corporations don't go looking outside to fill an executive secretary opening. They move up a secretary from within when they need one.

*   *   *   *   *

Today RK finally telephoned his son. But never mentioned he's dying. Told Junior of a new marketing plan he wanted him to present to the board at the next meeting. Junior is vice president, marketing. That's his title. But RK is really in charge of marketing just as he's in charge of everything else. Typical of RK, he told Junior exactly what he wanted for the new plan. Spelled it out in great detail. I hope Junior got it all. A big expansion internationally. Lots of start-up projects to enter more markets in more places around the world, all costing enough to impact earnings for at least the next two years. Not once did RK ask Junior what he thought. Junior is really just his flunky. And Junior offered no suggestions, asked for no changes. But then Junior is a playboy. A nice wife he doesn't deserve and three children. Only forty-five. Good looking but with nothing like his father's imposing presence, his build, his stance, his majestic head. Especially not his father in brains and drive. Lazy actually. Junior certainly could not glean any change in his father from that phone conversation. When will RK start telling his son and the others?

Now I suddenly guess what RK probably is up to! He's going to make Junior his successor! Now, that really frightens me! RK has phoned the five outside directors and told them about the new marketing plan — that the company's products are fine, ahead of or better than competition, but we've been too conservative in marketing, especially in international marketing. Claimed it was his own fault. We should expand our marketing worldwide — set up more overseas sales offices — do more advertising — and double sales. Said Junior will explain it all at the next board meeting. World marketing is going to be the big company drive, the key company strategy change for the next five years. So, in other words, without mentioning it, he has started the directors thinking that the president, Lon Larsen, who is actually only his finance and accounting assistant, is not the right man to be the next CEO. Neither is Will Miller, the V.P. for operations, who is concerned only with getting the products out. Marketing is now the big priority and, well, Junior is supposedly the number one marketing executive. RK, I think now, is planning to build up Junior in the months ahead starting with Junior presenting that big marketing expansion plan to the board. RK will lay out all the charts for Junior to use and RK will write the text and then rehearse Junior on his presentation. RK knows Junior's limitations. Never has he shown Junior any father-son warmth. But now that he's dying, I guess he wants his only son, his blood, to inherit and run the company he built.

Today RK took a big step. He had me put out two short announcements, one for the outside and one for the inside. Both said he would retire from the company at his next birthday just four months away, that a special committee of outside board members will commence the search for his successor as CEO, and that the choice might be either a present officer or someone from the outside. Before the announcement was released he read it on the phone to the outside directors and, while talking to them, he reminded them that the big new marketing expansion plan would be presented by Junior at the next board meeting. I know he did that to keep both the marketing issue and Junior at the top of their minds. He said nothing about his illness, not a hint. So, they still think he's going to live forever, just the way he himself used to think. RK knew what he was doing. The board always rubber-stamps anything he wants to do. Why not? He's always had everything covered. He's never made mistakes. At least none they could notice when they only show up for a half-day's board meeting once every three months. All they know is that the company is very profitable, and is growing, with no real troubles. Everything is decided for them by a powerhouse of a CEO. They get their generous director's fees and the pleasure and prestige of being on RK's board and they've had no worries. They will figure that if things do not go well after he retires he will step back in. They will guess he will really not be retired, only appear to be. The biggest shareholder by far, he would never allow himself to be ignorant of what is happening. So they'll let him appoint anyone he chooses as CEO, even Junior. In a year, after RK is gone and the directors recover from their shock, they will realize RK made an awful mistake — puts Junior into the CEO job and then goes and dies on them. Meanwhile, my problem is here and now. I have spoken the absolute minimum of words to Junior in over twenty years. Ever since that dumb thing I did six weeks after I joined the company. Well, it was not so much dumb as naïve. Of course, to be honest, I didn't have to do it. Fresh from my divorce, on my first job, and here the only son of the company's Supergod begins paying all that attention to me. I actually thought he had fallen hard for me. I even imagined that we would marry. For maybe a week or so I did. Then all the other young secretaries informed me that it was his goal to make it with every good-looking girl in the company before his first year in the company was over and that he was half way through the list when he got to me. But at least I came to my senses after I saw his attitude in the days that followed that one night. He never got another chance with me. He tried but I cut him off. Finally, I guess he accepted that we would have only the least to do with one another, only what company business might require. RK surely was never aware that I had once slept with his son. I worried about that when RK told me I was to be his secretary. Then quickly I learned he didn't see his son or talk to him except at the company, and that almost entirely by telephone, as RK did with everyone. RK didn't care what Junior did in his private life. What if Junior — after he gets the CEO job — asks me to stay on as his secretary? It would make sense because I know a lot that would help him. Come to think of it, does he even remember ever having sex with me, what with the number of secretaries over the years and all the pick-ups and the others? Oh, he remembers all right. He knows why I've been cold and short with him all these years I've been running RK's office. Maybe he thinks I'm just efficient, busy. Who knows? Who cares? Because I'm not going to be his secretary. When RK leaves the company, I'll leave too.

This crazy thing RK is doing is keeping me awake a lot of the night — RK setting up for Junior to be accepted as CEO by the outside board members — RK telling no one he is dying. The company's stock price went up after RK's retirement announcement. Everyone thinks that an aging, long-in-place CEO must by now be missing something about the changing world. No matter how good the CEO's been, there's a time for him to go. Meanwhile the retirement announcement is causing a furor internally because no successor was named in the announcement. So the three top insiders, Junior on marketing, Lon Larsen, the president, but really just financial man, and Will Miller on operations — all three are being assumed candidates. Some are saying it will be an outsider because if RK wanted an insider he would already have known which one and that person would have been named in the announcement. It's puzzling to me that I've picked up no gossip about people inside ruling out Junior. Could it be that they really don't know how incompetent he is, how RK has really been running marketing, much more even than he's been running the financial area and the operations?

Now I have a new big bother. Lon Larsen just called me here at home and told me, very confidentially he said, that he expects to be named to succeed RK as CEO. He said he doubts the directors will find it preferable to go outside and that surely neither Miller nor Junior could be taken seriously by the directors as a CEO. Besides, he said, he is the president of the company, has worked most closely with RK, and RK is merely retiring not dying — I bit my lip when I heard that — so RK, he said, will keep his oar in. Larsen therefore figures things won't be all that different. RK, he stated confidently, would never put a stranger from the outside in the CEO post. That person would expect to count RK as finished and out, and RK would know that — and so on and on. All this very awkward for me to listen to because Larsen should not be telling me these things and I can't say anything in return. Especially since all this time I naturally am assuming that he's really calling me to fish — to see what he can learn from me about RK's choice. Since I'm RK's secretary, it's totally out of order for me to be in such a discussion with him and he knows it. But it turns out that he is calling me because, when he gets the job, as he seems sure he will, he says he wants me to be his secretary. Says he'll need me and he is giving me the information now so I won't make other plans. I say nothing in response except to thank him for thinking of me. Now I'm the one that has to do a lot of thinking. Of course I'd sooner see Larsen than Junior as the next CEO. If Larsen should be in, then I will still have my job. But he's dreaming because there's something very wrong here. Can I do something about it all? It's not my place, I know, but should I do something anyway? What can I do?

I know something I could do. But it's even worse than my getting hooked on eavesdropping. So I won't do it. Still, I can't get it out of my mind now that I see what I could do. The way to avert the catastrophe — RK making Junior his successor — is for the outside board members to learn that RK is deathly ill. If they knew he soon will die then they will not give Junior the company to run. For the first time since they became board of directors members they will have a crisis to handle. They will be shocked when they hear RK won't be around. They will have to make the transformation almost instantly from sanguine yes men to concerned and responsible directors. And what's the easiest way for me to let them know? I simply call one of them, give him the bad news, and he will call the others. Fred Rogers would be the one to call. He's the oldest director, one all the other directors like and respect. What am I thinking? It would strike him instantly as very peculiar that I am the one calling him with such news. It isn't the job of a secretary to the CEO to convey information that the boss is dying to a director, unless the boss has asked her to do so. But Rogers would know that couldn't be the case because if RK wanted it done, he would do the telling himself. The first thing Rogers would do is phone RK, because he would wonder why I was acting so strangely. He for sure would ask RK what's really up about his health. Then RK would tell him the truth and the other directors would be told in no time. Of course, RK would be furious with me. He might fire me. He should. But Junior would not end up with the CEO job. I would have accomplished that, but I would really have messed up my own life. My relationship with RK would be severed in the last few months of his life. No. I can't do it. But, I could tell Larsen about RK's inoperable tumor. That would be easier because Larsen took the initiative in talking to me. Larsen wanting the job and thinking he has it — what would he do? He doesn't even know about RK's plan to elevate Junior. Well, if I'm going to tell Larsen about RK's situation, I might just as well tell him about how RK is planning to have Junior succeed him. All this is beginning to sound like a coup against RK and his son, with me as the instigator. Again, I'd surely be fired by RK. He would be disappointed in me, mad at me. Larsen surely would go to work on the directors and try to pin down the job for himself. But with RK still CEO and wanting Junior to succeed him, he might fire Larsen. Wait a minute. Larsen would think that possibility out ahead of time, before he did anything. He's not dumb. So what would he really do if I told him RK was soon to be gone? Maybe he would merely protect himself. Yes, that's it. He would not call the outside directors at all. Instead, he would go to RK, tell him what I had said, ask for corroboration, ask how he could help RK. Then RK would know he must now disclose his predicament to all directors. Maybe the directors, seeing they must now rise to the occasion, would come see RK to discuss CEO candidates seriously. Maybe RK would be made to realize that he is wrong in trying to arrange for Junior to replace him and they would all agree on Larsen. If I have already been dismissed by RK, would Larsen bring me back to be his secretary? Of course not. Larsen would be occupying the post before RK's death, in that last period when RK could no longer come to the office. Even if he thought I would be valuable because of what I know, it would be too awkward to rehire me. Besides, how could Larsen trust me? What might I tell others about him without his permission if that's the kind of thing I do? So, what does it all add up to? I've invented various ways to keep Junior out of the top job, but they all require that I ruin my life in the process!

In bed at 4:30 this morning I reached the conclusion that there was something I really could and should do, even though it seemed half crazy, and I wasn't sure I really would do it when tomorrow came. When I reached the office my brain felt frozen. RK arrived, gave me his regular nod and smile but, unlike his usual pattern, did not rattle off six or seven names of people he wanted me to get right away on the phone. He seemed to start to, then he stopped and said he'd buzz me in a minute. I gave him five minutes then opened his door, half expecting him to be in his lavatory. He was sitting at his desk — no papers on it, his hands folded, staring out the window. He turned to me. I started to say something but my voice was so faint it scared me and I stopped after I said "Mr. Reese,

I need to talk to you." I was petrified. I could see that he knew something was wrong with me because he told me to sit down. I started again. "Mr. Reese, I listened in on the call from the doctor at Mayo. I know I shouldn't have, but I did." He just looked at me with no expression. Then he said "Why?" I hadn't expected that question and I said the first thing that came to my mind. "Because I was worried about you." And then he said "No — not why did you listen in. Why are you telling me that you listened, that you know?" And now again I was shocked because it was a surprising question. I felt I was going to collapse with nervousness, with the realization that I was engaged in totally idiotic behavior — this coming into his office, sitting down, getting into a conversation with him about personal things, that I had never talked with him about, and now I found I really didn't have a thought-out plan. It had seemed like I had a plan in the middle of last night, but now I was like a frightened child lost in a strange, scary place. Then, I just let go and rattled off that he was doing the wrong thing, that he ought to be home resting and not at the office, that he should be telling his directors and his son about his condition, that he owed it to them and his employees and stock holders. When I finally ran out of words, I saw him looking at me calmly — kindly, tenderly. I had not ever seen that look before. He was often nice to me, complimented me when I handled something especially well. But this look told me he saw my anguish and forgave my frenzied utterances and he actually said "I understand." Then he shocked me by saying that he had planned that very day to disclose to only a few why he was retiring, to be followed by an announcement a day or two later. Soon it would be known to all, he said. He was sure that he would remain strong enough to see that the company's new marketing drive had been well started.

That would be his last contribution and it was very important. Then he said he now planned to quickly settle the matter of succession. He said, with emphasis, that of course no one internally could do the CEO task anywhere near the level of competence the job required. It was his fault that no successor had been groomed, ready to take over. Yet he was not sorry, he said, that he had created no understudy. He was a hands-on manager. He had to be in direct control. No top man from outside would take the job just because he announced his retirement, he said, because they would all assume he would be around, over-seeing, interfering, using his reputation and big block of shares and his detailed knowledge of the company to intimidate the new CEO. There were several outstanding executives in other companies that he had explored, he told me, and he would now choose one. He had had to wait to approach them until it could be made clear to them that he would not remain around. Then he said he was telling me all this for a special reason and not just to calm me down. Everyone, he said, naturally will soon be wondering what will happen to his shares in the company. Promoters on the outside can be counted on to see an opportunity to try to grab control of the company and manipulate it so as to get a financial short term gain. So he has to be careful what he does. Well, he said, he is not going to leave his shares to Junior. Junior, he then said, suffers from permanent immaturity and if given the stock would either dissipate the fortune quickly or use the voting power to drive the new CEO crazy. No. Instead, he will contribute his stock to a half dozen universities. Then he looked at me — again with that special new look of affection — and said the new CEO will doubtless want to bring in his own assistant. He would particularly not want RK's assistant because she would always be thinking about how RK operated. But he wanted me to be secure for the rest of my life and he hoped I would have a very long life. So he said he is arranging for me a life annuity, the income of which will take care of me very well. And then he stood up and that meant the meeting was over. And I said "I don't know what to say" and he said, "Thank you will be just right, and you can then get back to your work."

Chapter 8: Rules of Behavior

"Vern, I've got a bad problem, one I've got to handle immediately. It sure would help if I could come talk to you."

"Can you come down right now, Cliff? I'm preparing for a luncheon meeting, but I'll stop that."

"Trouble is, Vern, I have to stay by this phone. Can you come up here? I'll give you lunch."

"Yes. I'll shift my meeting 'till after lunch. It's an internal Branton session and my managers will adjust, Cliff. I'll be up in ten minutes."

Clifford Mather and Vernon Walberg had been each other's best friend since the Walbergs bought the house next door to the Mathers when the two boys were fourteen. They did everything together. Each excelled at math, was a fast runner, and played in the band. They planned their futures together. Both got degrees in chemical engineering, followed by M.B.A.'s at the state university, and then accepted job offers at Universal Chemtek, the biggest company in their Midwest town.

At UniChem, both were quickly pegged as comers. One of them, everyone said early on, was sure one day to become the company's chief executive. Of course, the two friends themselves would talk about their eventual competition for the top job at UniChem. Sometimes they joked about it, but mostly those conversations were serious. They agreed they must work together to ensure that no third, less deserving but perhaps more cunning, candidate would beat them out.

One of them, they decided, could end up as chairman of the board and the other as the president. They would be partners and neither would be unhappy if the other was nominally regarded as the higher boss.

As both moved up in the company, Vern began to notice that one conspicuous characteristic of Cliff's that had always made him wonderful as a friend was less than ideal for a successful top executive. Cliff was overly softhearted. He simply could not bear to hurt anyone. He would seek Vern's advice whenever he had to handle a disappointing performance by a subordinate.

Despite this shortcoming of Cliff's, he was very sharp and easily the most popular member of his age group in the company. Vern knew he could not match Cliff in the natural warmth he displayed to his associates so Vern knew Cliff might emerge as UniChem's chief executive. If Vern were then Cliff's key deputy, Vern would be playing the bad cop role to Cliff's good cop. Vern hated the thought of acquiring the image of being coldly efficient and always having to do the dirty work.

It might be equally bad, Vern would imagine, if he were made the CEO and Cliff the next highest company officer under him. Cliff would always be coming to Vern to take over those necessary actions that might offend, disturb, or harm any employee. And, Vern would never be able to fire Cliff.

These thoughts of Vern fortunately lost their significance when he received a totally unexpected offer from Albert Branton, the founder and proprietor of Branton Batteries, to head that company. Branton's biggest product line was high capacity battery packs to furnish standby emergency power should the regular power supply fail. They were sold to hospitals, fire stations, police departments, telephone central stations, airports, and many other facilities. Vern, among his company assignments, had been UniChem's applications engineer on the Branton account, and Albert Branton had been extremely happy with the company's providing for his chemical needs. He was especially impressed with Vern.

Having had one severe heart attack already, Branton, still in his sixties, began seeking a young man to be his successor. Vern accepted the offer on the understanding that profits would be plowed back for several years to broaden the business. Vern wanted to produce Diesel generator systems and all the associated control apparatus. Albert Branton could elect to follow this expansion strategy because, as the sole owner, he did not have to please other shareholders by maximizing short-term earnings. Vern also wanted to go after defense department business, such as rugged emergency power systems for naval ships, and, at the other extreme, to mass manufacture power installations for small facilities like offices of doctors and dentists that wanted to be certain of electricity under all circumstances.

Thus Vern became the chief executive of what was soon renamed Branton Industries and that grew to be a billion-dollar company listed on the New York stock exchange. Meanwhile, Cliff reached the top at Universal Chemtek. Both companies eventually set up their corporate executive offices in the newest and tallest building in the city. Vern and Cliff joined each other's board of directors and lunched in each other's offices very frequently.

Cliff seldom drank and Vern hardly ever had a cocktail before dinnertime. But when offered a drink by Cliff immediately on arriving for lunch, Vern sensed it would be best to join Cliff. Cliff swallowed his quickly and got right to his problem.

"Ed Greer got a call yesterday telling him to be at the White House this afternoon to discuss his becoming

Secretary of Labor and maybe seeing the President tomorrow morning. Ed's name, as I'm sure you've noted, has been mentioned for that job. On this visit — if he does indeed meet with the President — that means he'll be asked to take the post."

"And that bothers you?"

"Yes, Vern, it does, very much."

"Why? Surely it's not for the usual reason."

"What's the usual reason?"

"I mean the standard, Republican, big-business, co-operative plan for staffing the Executive Department, Cliff. When a Democrat takes over the White House, we business leaders of the nation are scared to death that anti-business policies will dominate every federal office. So the industry CEOs work at getting business people we trust into as many appointive slots as possible. But the really good executives usually can't be spared. That means the industry guys offered up have personal problems, or mediocre ability, or bad lungs — lots of things that make them wrong for the appointments."

"Stop exaggerating, Vern," Cliff replied.

"O.K. Cliff, so I'm exaggerating. Yes. Competent people sometimes do leave big jobs in business to go take government posts. But they sure aren't pushed into it by their bosses in industry. They happen to be people who want to help their country and who actually merit the assignments."

"Yes, Vern — but now a Republican is in the White House. So what is it we patriotic board chairmen do?"

"Oh, well, then the CEO's are not at all worried. After all, the Republican party is us. Of course, we're still called upon by the White House to suggest names, experienced executives who know how to organize a task, how to make and stick to a budget. Still, it's a golden opportunity to foist off on Washington all our problem cases. Yes, a few great guys show up here and there — as exceptions."

This was said with diminished emphasis, because Vern now realized his facetiousness was adding to Cliff's disturbed state, whatever was causing it, and that he must hasten to get the subject redirected.

"Cliff, old pal, I know <u>you</u> would not be dumping on the President a lemon, a has-been, problem case. And, look, everyone knows your man Ed Greer is a prime candidate for the labor secretary. He's got a national reputation, so well known for his labor problem solving expertise that I doubt you had to suggest him. Your personal patriotism would make you willing to get along without him if the nation needs him in the Secretary's job. So what's the problem here?"

There was a pause. Cliff looked at his watch, then said slowly and quietly: "Vern, I didn't suggest Ed Greer for that job. I expect Ed to call me any minute to report on his White House meeting. I hope to God he hasn't seen the President. If he has, and I've been too late, then I've been derelict in my duties as a good citizen."

Vern stared at Cliff with surprise.

"Cliff, did Ed say he would accept the job if offered? Does he want to go to Washington? What's so wrong about that?"

"I'll tell you. Several weeks ago, Vern, I had a very painful talk with Ed. It was before any word had come out about the Administration's being interested in him, so the timing of our conversation had nothing to do with that. He might have thought about it afterward and thought I had some advance knowledge that he would be a candidate for the President's cabinet and that that was why I chose to talk to him. But I didn't have a clue about a Washington appointment then. Anyway, Vern, I told Ed Greer, our national labor luminary, my executive most widely known on the outside, that he has become an alcoholic. I told him he must grab hold of it, go see a doctor at a clinic I named, and absolutely and totally stop all drinking."

The real conversation, thought Vern, probably had been somewhat different from what Cliff's brisk summary described. Cliff had probably only hinted at alcoholism. Maybe he said he was worried about Ed's becoming an alcoholic someday. The conversation would have been painful for Cliff. If Ed was inclined not to face the problem, if he had forced a strong, unequivocal comment from Cliff, then it must have been a difficult conversation indeed for his good friend.

Some years before, Ed Greer had been an unknown number two man at corporate level in labor relations at UniChem. His boss, Guy Simmons, had done only a so-so job in dealing with union leaders. Mostly, he had gone about giving speeches at the company's plants. A bit of that would have been o.k., but his style and content and his repertoire of clichés were unsuited to the times. Ed Greer had carried the main load of keeping the company's unions and employees happy.

Then a serious labor battle started in a nearby company and quickly spread to other companies and even to Universal Chemtek. Whatever the beginning issue, the strikes developed multiple fronts — wage increases, of course, protections against layoff, pension policies, whites versus blacks, and various unions versus each other. With strikes, sit-downs, plant closings, and then arson and riots, a broad industrial area was threatened with chaos. The strikes made the front pages all over the nation. The mayors of the involved cities and the governor of the state talked of martial law.

Then, the confusion and agony began to diminish. Issues were articulated, attacked, and negotiated. One man emerged as the conceiver and arranger of the positive steps — a master in pleading, convincing, and leading — Ed Greer.

Greer was labeled a hero. He appeared on the cover of Time and was interviewed on the Today show. In the following year, because he was so heavily importuned to make Greer available, Cliff Mather let Greer tackle outside labor issues. He would be sought as a neutral, objective, and expert project head to straighten out various nasty labor problems. He was even pulled in by the Governor of far-off California to propose ways acceptable to the feuding unions and farm owners to improve the lot of migrant farm workers.

Finally, Simmons reached mandatory retirement age at Universal Chemtek and Ed Greer became the vice president for labor relations, the job he had been performing brilliantly for years without the title. If Ed now has taken to drink, Vern thought, it would not be surprising. He had long been under immense pressure, operating on impossible schedules, violence often a threat.

"I know all the signs," said Cliff. "I've seen enough of it with family and friends and business associates. Of course, only some people are highly addictive to alcohol. It takes a combination of things, not just physical susceptibility — a personal frustration or dilemma, a powerful need for whatever it is that alcohol seems at first to do for that individual, a lack of realization of the developing pattern by the drinker. I've never been wrong in spotting an alcoholic."

"How long has Ed Greer been an alcoholic?"

"I've been sure of it for months. Yet, I don't know that anyone else would call him an alcoholic."

"You mean other company people haven't noticed?"

"They would maybe say he's a heavy drinker but that he can hold his liquor. But he has begun to skip management meetings he is supposed to attend here first thing in the morning. I've known that he can't get up for them after an evening when I've seen him put away too much. I've covered for him. Two weeks ago, Ed's wife woke me, very apologetically, saying she had expected him home for dinner and here it was 1:00 a.m. and no call and no Ed. I'm sure something like that had happened earlier. She wouldn't have awakened me if it had been the first time. She was scared."

"So, you're afraid that Ed will become the labor secretary," said Vern, "and will go on drinking, and that he's an alcoholic will become evident. Tell me, Cliff, what has you so disturbed? It's not your losing an alcoholic team member. Are you thinking about your personal discomfort should high-level Administration officials come back at you for not telling them? Are you worried mostly about the nation if you let an alcoholic onto the President's cabinet?"

"Damn it, Vern, I'm worried now about everyone and everything, including Ed himself. I mishandled it. I should have brought it up to the Administration when I first learned they were thinking about him for the job. I counted on Ed turning it down. After all, I had warned him. But he didn't accept that he is an alcoholic. Then, too, hell, I figured that no one else was telling on him. You've already mentioned the hypocrites in big business, the leaders of corporations — how we pawn off our problem executives. Here you have the whole industrial labor world believing Ed is <u>the</u> man for the job, and then, what? I come along and announce he's an alcoholic and should not be in the cabinet. Some might figure I just didn't want to lose him, or that I'm a pompous, temperance zealot or something.

All I really have, Vern, is my personal conviction that soon he'll be out of control. I can't prove it."

"What about the FBI, Cliff? Don't they always send out a team to interrogate every candidate's associates before they finalize a federal appointment? You know — they ask everyone about personal habits, associations, drinking, sex deviations, and national disloyalty — the whole works."

"Sure they investigate. The FBI questioned me. You know what I told the FBI? That he drinks the way many busy people under a lot of pressure do, who have a heavy schedule of decision meetings and crises and too many receptions and banquets and little time for themselves."

"I remember, Cliff, when they investigated me before a government appointment I had accepted. It was just to be a member of a temporary White House advisory committee. The FBI asked my neighbors if there appeared to be an undue number of liquor bottles in my garbage."

"Yes, Vern, but they would expect the trash can of a vice president for labor relations of a large company to contain not just bottles, but empty cases. Anyway, to put it bluntly, but accurately, when it comes to Ed's drinking, I was silent. Several times I was on the verge of calling someone to inject the truth, and each time I couldn't bring myself to do it. Now, take our friend Eli Murphy, our state's biggest Republican businessman. If he, by magic, had taken over my brain when I first learned Ed was being considered, he would have called the White House and put in the word that Ed Greer has a drinking problem, and that would have stopped the whole appointment process. If Ed, or anyone else, had then complained to Eli, he'd have told them to go to hell, that he was doing everyone a favor by his straight action. He would have been on a new problem at the end of fifteen minutes and could have then given me back my brain.

"Well, Vern, I thought about Eli, how he'd handle it, but I did nothing. To tell you the truth, I hoped the White House would choose some other candidate. But Ed is damned attractive. He's really the only big corporation labor man you could put in that job and have it bought by labor enthusiastically. With Ed as Secretary, the President could put a labor union leader in as Undersecretary. Then he'd have a two-man team that could really handle Congress, business, labor unions, the media, the public, and all a hell of a lot better than it has ever been done. Anyway, when Ed called me and said he was heading for Washington and would phone after his White House meeting, I really began to squirm."

"So, Cliff, I'll bet you did call Eli for an assist on stopping the nomination."

"Exactly, Vern. I had let it go too long. Now I couldn't stop it myself. Just imagine the headlines: Big business boss of proposed labor secretary claims leading candidate is an alcoholic. Well, I called Eli and told him the story. I pleaded with him, what with his friendship with the President, to get to him before the public announcement, hopefully still a day away. I asked him to say, 'Mr. President, I have some information I would prefer not to discuss that forces me to call and say that I recommend that you don't make Greer your new labor secretary.' That would end it. Eli said he would do it immediately. He told me he didn't think he would have to elaborate but, if he were forced to, he would tell the truth, that Greer's employer, mentioning my name, an ethical man who should know, says Greer is an alcoholic."

Eli Murphy had that position with the President, Vern knew. Cliff, like Vern, had shaken the President's hand once or twice in a large group, but Murphy, a truly big fundraiser for the party, was seeing the President regularly.

"So, Cliff — did Eli reach the President?"

"Eli said he would call me as soon as he did. If he had gotten through, I'm sure he would have phoned me by now to tell me what he said and what the President said. I guess I'll hear from Eli or Ed very soon. It's a tossup which one will report first and I'm nervous as hell."

The question seemed resolved, however, in the very next moment. Cliff's secretary called Cliff and announced that Mr. Greer was calling.

"Shift the call in here, please, Mrs. Ames."

The conversation was exceedingly brief, with Cliff saying only a "Hello, Ed" and "Uh huh" a few times and then "Congratulations, Ed — come in to see me as soon as you get back."

Hearing this Vern feared the worst, especially since Cliff looked flabbergasted.

"Ed is going to be Undersecretary, not Secretary, Vern! Ed said he told the White House people that while he'd like to be Secretary he couldn't accept because his doctor told him he would not be able to stand the pressure. Ed suggested they take their top labor union candidate, Harold Karechi, and make him Secretary, and, if Karechi would approve of having Ed as his deputy, Ed said he would be most anxious to try to help the country all he can in that lesser responsibility post. Karechi, it turned out, was also at the White House because they had planned to settle both jobs today, only the other way around, Karechi as Undersecretary to Ed's Secretary. And Ed says they've talked it all out. They took the plan to the President and he approved. Everyone is enthusiastic. Tomorrow they will appear with the President in front of the TV cameras as he announces the two appointments."

Cliff blurted it all out in virtually one breath, still looking stunned.

"Quick, Cliff," said Vern. "There's a loose end. It's important! Get Eli Murphy on the phone and tell him to cancel his call to the President."

"Oh, my God, yes, Vern! Let's get back to my office."

They hurried down the hall and Mrs. Ames placed the call. Murphy's secretary reported that Murphy was on his way back from a luncheon meeting and was expected any moment. Cliff left explicit instructions with Mrs. Ames to tell Mr. Murphy's secretary that, please, Murphy must not take a call from the White House should it come in. It was absolutely imperative, Mr. Murphy's secretary must understand, that Mr. Murphy should talk to Mr. Mather first. She said she would see to that. Cliff settled back to wait. He looked at Vern and put his two hands together under his chin in a praying posture.

"Well! That was a close one, Cliff. It's not absolutely over yet, but I think you'll catch Murphy in time."

"I was saved, Vern, if indeed I have been, by Ed's good sense, not mine."

"Now, wait a minute, Cliff. You talked to Ed Greer about his drinking and you were honest with him. That took courage. But you did it. We now know that Ed took your comments to heart. He acted on your advice. Maybe he resisted, or was shocked even, when you first spoke up as you did. But then your message began to penetrate his mind. Your message, remember that — no one else's. So relax, Cliff. You took the correct, forthright action. Sure, if Ed had ignored your remarks and accepted the appointment as Secretary, and then had turned out to be a major public and Administration embarrassment, and you had let it happen — yes, then you would have cause to regret your inaction. Cliff, you did what was fitting after all."

They were interrupted by the call from Murphy. Again the conversation was brief.

"Well, Vern, you heard what I just said. When I told Eli what the score now was with Ed, he immediately said, even before I could suggest it, 'Fine, I'll cancel my call to the President.' Eli remarked that if the President should return his call he would give the President some advice on something else. 'He can always stand some more advice from me, you know,' Eli said. Eli didn't chide me for getting him involved in the whole matter needlessly. I didn't have to explain anything."

"So, Cliff. Here you go again. You've straightened out Ed Greer, who probably will never ever touch a drop of liquor again. You've helped the nation get what will probably be its strongest Labor Department leadership ever — all this without hurting anyone. A perfect illustration, a perfect execution, of the Clifford Mather rules of behavior. The story of your life. May I now go back to my office and start the meeting you made me delay?"

"Of course. And I thank you, Vernon — once again. There's just one thing."

"Yes — what?"

"If Ed was so wrong for the Secretary slot because of his drinking why is he so safe for Undersecretary? That's not a trivial position. Should I do something, say something, to someone?"

"Oh no you don't! You're not getting me into that. Not today, Clifford. Not two of your problems a day, my friend. That would violate a Vernon Walberg rule of behavior."

Chapter 9: Politics Anonymous

Of all billion-dollar corporations, Portran, Inc. probably has the most modest corporate headquarters. Some attribute CEO Frank Abbott's disinterest in front office elegance to his once having been a truck driver. They suspect his present office to be not much different from the one he used when, early in his twenties, he first launched his trucking firm.

"Big Frank" Abbott wasn't called big anything in the beginning. He was just a stocky, tough-looking young man with obvious energy and guts. He persuaded other single truck owners to band with him and go for large contracts. He talked customers into assignments beyond what he was prepared to handle, then used the contracts to secure bank loans to cover leasing more trucks in a hurry, and was always on time with his committed customer service and his interest payments. He aggressively exploited his earnings record and credit rating to borrow avidly and expand by buying up competitive trucking outfits.

In a few years he took over a nation-wide trucking firm with more than a thousand trucks and not long afterwards an even larger company, a distribution outfit operating worldwide. Abbott Trucking became Portran, Inc., rose past $500 million in annual revenues, went public and was listed on the stock exchanges. His body weight expanded with his operations and he became known as Big Frank.

Harold Webster joined Portran's board of directors somewhat by accident. He had merged his Webster

Furniture Stores with the Hamilton Retail Group. Hamilton had consisted of two entities, one its furniture outlets and the other a large shipping firm Webster did not want and sold to Portran. Big Frank insisted that the deal include Webster's joining Portran's board, thinking this would yield to Portran the substantial trucking business of Hamilton-Webster. But Webster always looked for the best deal for Hamilton-Webster and was unwilling to favor Portran. That was one of a number of substantial annoyances Big Frank felt with Webster as a Portran board member. Both knew the association was not likely to be long lasting.

Portran's headquarters building was really only a crude fronting structure added onto an old warehouse set back from the street. When Harold Webster and his fellow director Henry Donaldson entered the small lobby, the receptionist pushed an intercom button and Abbott's secretary quickly came to escort them to his office. They walked along a narrow hall with faded carpeting on the floor, its walls lined with cheap wood paneling decorated with Portran corporate advertisements in dull brown plastic frames.

Webster steeled himself for the boisterous greeting he knew Abbott would soon provide. Big Frank, thought Webster, could play the role of a ward politician in a B-movie with minimum direction. And, indeed, here came the hippopotamus, steaming out of his office, his left hand extended to one director, his right to the other, both arms set to pump vigorously and then deliver forceful pats on the backs.

"So — my two senior directors, Web and Henry — both looking terrific — except —— Web looking grumpy and Henry, my perpetually quiet director, looking even more quiet than usual. Come on in!"

As they settled into their chairs, Big Frank was beaming with the zestful look of a hungry man sitting down at a table laden with his favorite food. Henry Donaldson, Web noted, was being careful not to look directly into the eyes of either of them, oscillating in his gaze between the floor and the map on one wall of the small, crowded office. It was embellished with little pinned flags showing locations of Portran facilities in North America and Europe.

Web was not surprised that Henry could not hide his unhappiness at being present. It was 9:30 that morning when Web told Henry on the phone what Marshall Lee, a Portran vice-president, had told him late the evening before. Henry was a man of the highest ethics in business, and so reserved in manner that Web knew people could be forgiven for thinking his friend a milquetoast. Although Henry possessed legal education, he would be of limited help in confronting Big Frank with the problem Lee had disclosed. Web knew immediately from Henry's choice of words on the phone that he was disturbed to hear what Lee had claimed. Especially awesome to Henry, Web was aware, was Henry's realization that he might have to get involved. Henry hated un-pleasantries.

Donaldson Metals had been started by an ancestor of Henry's during the Civil War to make nuts and bolts. Last year the company mass-produced over a hundred million dollars worth of metal fasteners, snaps, rivets, nuts, bolts, bearings, brackets, zippers, clamps, nails, washers, clips, and small gears. In recent years the company had been in the hands of Henry's older brother, Douglas, who had been trained for the job. His deceased father had planned that Henry would help his brother run the family company as its lawyer but thought Henry too gentle to be an executive. But five years into his tenure, Douglas suddenly succumbed to a heart attack and Henry, unprepared and shocked, found himself inheriting the position of Chairman and Chief Executive of Donaldson Metals.

"Now, Henry," Web had reported in his morning call, "I'll admit I don't know whether Marshall Lee told me the whole truth last night. And frankly, I'm not clear why Lee would put himself in this position — I mean, telling me, a Portran director, let alone planning to tell the FBI, something so self-incriminating and, of course, so disastrous to Big Frank and Portran."

"You find it believable that Big Frank has been acting crazy?"

"Yes, Henry. I can understand Big Frank doing this kind of thing. Look, we know about his vigorous interest in owning politicians. And his absolute self-confidence. He probably figured it could never come out or, if it did, that he could deny it and get away with it. I don't know. But in any case, don't you see, Henry, we have got to go to Big Frank, tell him what Lee has said, and hear how he responds?"

"Web, why don't you just phone Frank and tell him that Lee came to you and made these charges? You should do it without implying any judgments. Don't give him any reason to believe that you assume the charges are true."

"Wait a minute, Henry. You know that as directors we will be interrogated by the FBI after they hear from Lee, and later we might be before a grand jury. Whether Lee is telling the truth or not, this isn't something we dismiss with a phone call."

"Web, you know I'm not any good at this sort of thing. I don't know anything about this illegal political contribution business of Big Frank's. It's going to be totally believable — I mean, to either the FBI or a grand Jury — that whatever Big Frank has been up to that's illegal he didn't share it with the directors. He certainly didn't share it with me. I'll simply tell the truth, if asked, that I know nothing."

"Come now, Henry. Who is good at this kind of thing? Lee did come to me with his story and I have told it to you. When you're asked what you did, what action you took, when you heard about this, do you want to have to confess that you never even asked the Chairman of the Board whether he was guilty of the felonies his own vice-president accused him of? You know — aside from the FBI and the Securities and Exchange Commission — there's something else to consider: We might be sued later by the shareholders."

"All right, you bastards," said Frank, rocking in his huge desk chair and still smiling. The smile pained Web as much as Henry's visible embarrassment did. "I know you didn't come here to discuss Portran's contribution to the city's symphony orchestra. I know you two well enough to know you're not going to demand my resignation because Portran's earnings dropped a little last quarter. So what is it that brings both of you to see me — on demand — with no notice? It had to be today, you said, Web. Okay, what — what — what?"

"Your vice president for public relations, Marshall Lee, insisted on coming to my home yesterday evening, Frank," began Web. "He said it was an urgent matter. He didn't say it had anything to do with Portran. But it turns out it did, very much so — with Portran and with you, Frank."

Big Frank turned off his smile without moving a muscle of his body. With his lips almost closed he said quietly, "Cut the crap — I'm not playing games with you, Web — what the hell did he say? Why don't you just give me one of your succinct summaries — the way you do in board meetings when you don't like something I'm doing — which is too damned much of the time."

Web did exactly that. Despite Big Frank's tone, Web provided, with poise, a cogent recital of Lee's accusations.

This included that Lee planned to make the same statements to the FBI on Monday of next week when the FBI was scheduled to make its regular annual exam of political contributions by Portran and its officers. As Web spoke, Big Frank did not move although his lips stiffened. He looked directly into Web's eyes, paying no attention to Henry, whose face had begun to turn pinkish as Web spoke.

"That's it?" asked Frank, suddenly appearing relaxed and leaning far back in his chair. "Web, you and I are not really very compatible people, are we? We don't like each other. But I know you're telling me the truth. I mean, if you say this is what Marshall Lee told you, then it's what he told you. So, now I have to say to you that the man is a liar — and an ass-hole. I can guess why Lee has decided to do this crazy thing. It has to do with his crazy wife and that divorce he's going through — a shitty mess.

"But first," Big Frank continued, "let me say that for some years now my top executives and me — we've tried to see that the right things happen on the political front. Of our own choosing, using our privilege as citizens, we've been putting some of our own personal dollars where our mouths are. Do you know that the typical officer in American big business corporations — with a salary in the hundreds of thousands or millions of dollars a year — spends maybe a few thousand dollars backing up his political beliefs — maybe less — maybe nothing? Think of it. A piss-poor fraction of his pay! And then they bitch about how the politicians are fucking the country. Well, I happen to think, and my gang here at Portran agree with me, that ten percent is a little more like it. Putting our dough together, we've been donating well over a million bucks. That gives us some influence. Of course what we do is totally legal. We never make illegal contributions. This is our own money. Any questions yet? Web?"

"The FBI team will ask for cancelled checks. They'll want to see exactly how much was given to individual candidates, and that no Portran money went in," began Web.

"Exactly," interrupted Frank, "and they'll find the cancelled checks and the records all proper and complete. So I'm going to fire that goat-fucking Marshall Lee as soon as this meeting is over. But let's go on. You said that he claims I gave the donated money right back to my officers by issuing them salary bonuses of the amount of their contributions. Which is to say, I'm accused by Lee of hiding the fact that Portran has been making illegal political contributions.

"Let me see. Marshall Lee himself is not exactly one of our top people. But he's a two hundred thousand dollars-a-year man — that's for this last year that just ended — and that was made up of a hundred and fifty base pay and fifty of bonus. Now, you two are directors. You know we use that system of pay — base and bonus. Since you directors voted on his fifty thousand bonus, I wonder — you must be prepared to say under oath that you knew it was unearned, that it was just a way I thought up to shift Portran funds to political contributions. How could that be? You two saw the exact bonus for me and for every one of my staff. You approved the numbers, so I guess you believed they were the right compensations, considering everything, like what our competitors pay, our need to hold onto good men, our need to attract other top ones. I wouldn't want the job of a government lawyer — or a Marshall Lee for that matter — of trying to prove that somehow I made executives kick in to a political contribution pile that I controlled — and that I then reimbursed them all with Portran's shareholders' money by giving them undeserved bonuses. Should we go on? Or maybe you have some questions?"

Web motioned for Frank to continue by a wave of his hand. In response Frank performed an exaggerated fake courtesy gesture, putting one arm over his chest and bowing his heavy top torso, thinking he was being amusing.

"Now, let's see, what else did that prick Lee tell you? Oh yes — that I've used a consulting firm — Italian? — to launder illegal campaign funds. It's true that I've hired European consulting outfits to help me find good acquisitions. You two, you're directors — so you know that in the last several years, Portran has acquired some outstanding trucking firms in Europe — also a warehouse storage chain. You know we make our own studies of all possibilities, but we also use the banks over there and we employ various consultants. They're good. You can see detailed reports we get from them — they're in the files — data on companies and on market, economic, and political trends in various countries.

"Lee says — what? That I arranged for them to deliberately overcharge us and then secretly kick it all back? You'll find their services for us are carefully invoiced. Have those consultants been overcharging? I think not. Would they send what we send them back in small bills in a suitcase? Do you really want to go on with this meeting? Don't you want me to handle fucking fools when I discover them in my company? Do you really want to get further into this, Web? Christ, I know Henry here doesn't. Henry! Get your eyes off the goddamn ceiling and say something! You believe me, don't you, when I tell you there's nothing here that should worry you — as a director?"

"Frank," said Henry Donaldson, "you have to admit that when a vice president comes to an outside director and claims that the chairman of the board has been violating the law, then we have to come and tell you about it right away. Now that we've done that, I, for one, am perfectly willing to leave Lee's claims to you and the government to handle."

"Thank you, Henry. I appreciate your confidence," said Frank with a nod of his head. Then, turning to Web, his facial expression hardening, he went on to say, "And Web, the same I'm sure applies to your views now on this subject. True?"

"Frank" answered Web, "you know that if Marshall Lee tells the FBI what he said he would, they will launch a full investigation. They will question you and all your executives. They will go after your Italian consultants. They will ponder why Marshall Lee is willing to incriminate himself. They will talk to your protégé, Congressman Angus Fields, because Lee will tell them, as he told me, that Fields received most of your funds. This, Frank, is going to develop into one hell of a mess. As a director, I'm going to discharge my responsibilities. I am not going to walk away from it and leave it all to you — because you're the one being accused. It can't end with your firing Lee. In other words—"

"In other words, you don't belong on my board. On your way out, Mr. Webster, why don't you dictate a one-sentence letter of resignation? My secretary will be glad to type it right away for your signature. And that will end your service on the board and never being a team member. Then, you can do what you want about this Marshall Lee shit — and I'll do what I want. I'll take care of that shit-ass-prick Marshall Lee and his accusations and anything the FBI or anybody else wants to do about them. You'll be nothing more than a piss-pants nuisance on the side — a lot less so if I won't have to waste my time talking to you. Why the hell, Web, are you still sitting around?"

"Frank, don't be impatient. I'll leave because there is no point in my remaining in this meeting. But don't count on my resignation. I'm a director and I will do what I think I should do as a director."

Web rose and moved toward the door, deliberately not looking at Henry Donaldson.

"One moment, Mr. Webster," said Big Frank. "We're just beginning to draft the proxy statements and ballots for the election of board members at our next annual meeting. Don't expect your name to be on the slate I will offer the stockholders."

*   *   *   *   *

"Marshall, thanks for coming here right away this morning."

"Well, Web, I've got the time. Big Frank fired me yesterday. He said he also got rid of you, whatever that meant. You must have had quite a session."

"It was simple really, Marshall. Big Frank denied everything and told us to leave you to him and forget the matter. Henry Donaldson said he would and I said I wouldn't. That was when Big Frank quit being friendly. So I'm going to be a 'dissident' director until I'm voted out at the next shareholder's meeting. As I told him I would do, I'm going to take this situation seriously. I spent yesterday evening with my attorney —"

"Excuse me, Web," interrupted Marshall Lee, "I need to tell you something important that my attorney has suggested."

"It turns out" said Web "my attorney expressed some thoughts about you, Marshall. That's the reason I called you this morning and asked you to come by. He said that if he were your attorney he'd advise you not to tell the FBI anything next week. But you must not lie either. You should refuse to talk on the usual grounds it might incriminate you."

"Precisely. That's what my attorney said to do, Web. That would tell them there is something rotten in this situation that deserves their further investigation and they would report that to the Department of Justice and then --"

"Yes — and then you will agree to turn into a willing witness for the government in an immunity deal that lets you off practically free. I guess our attorneys agree. Have you decided to go with that approach?" asked Web.

"Yes, Web. My attorney is very optimistic about that route. He is sure the government will be after bigger fish. That means Big Frank, of course — and Congressman Angus Fields."

"But Marshall, my attorney called attention to a big problem. Big Frank has a simple story — how he and his executives put together a sum, totally legally, out of their own personal funds. Frank will claim no coercion by him took place and no Portran funds were in the act. Also, he will deny paying European consultants to do nothing but secretly give back virtually all the payments to him in cash.

"We have to assume also, Marshall, that the Italians will be very quiet. They can't be touched with felony charges over here and their admitting anything would merely put them in trouble with their own government on income tax evasion. They won't talk."

"Web," said Marshall Lee, "Frank Abbott told me two months ago to pick up four hundred thousand in cash from an Oliver Mason in the New York office of the Italian consulting firm and deliver it to Angus Fields in Washington. Oliver Mason is a Britisher on the payroll of the consulting firm. He lives in London."

"So unless you find Oliver Mason and he is willing to fess up and hurt himself" said Web, "you are an accuser with no proof. It will just be your word against that of Big Frank, a big political fund raiser, and against Angus Fields, a congressman."

"That's true, Web. But consider this — some twenty-five executives made contributions to Frank's political choices. Are all of them going to be good at lying? They will hear soon enough that I'm going to turn 'state's evidence.' I'm going to be prepared to spell out specific conversations where I told them how much in political donations to turn in to Big Frank. Some of them surely will be bothered about perjury before a grand jury. Of course, he can say my records were made up by me out of my imagination — but they will be helpful to a prosecuting attorney or an investigator. I'm not saying we've got easy proof against Big Frank. Just that there is a good chance that he or some of the others, in their answers to a grand jury, will cause that jury to doubt they're telling the truth.

"Another thing, Web. Big Frank is serious about pushing Angus Fields for the open Secretary of Labor slot. He wants Fields in the presidential cabinet for a couple of years and then he'll push him for the Senate. Fields is clever. He might be spectacular when he's quizzed by the Senate committee that has to approve cabinet appointees. If illegal campaign contributions come up he's sure to be spectacular, if he's a nominee for Labor Sec — even more spectacular than I guess I'm sure to be as a witness."

"If there's a possibility," said Web "that Fields will come soon before a Senate committee for approval as Secretary of Labor then that committee — and not a grand jury — that is where this whole Portran stink may first be aired — if you volunteer to testify. The Justice Department's lawyers might decide to let the Senate committee get into it first, and then pick up your accusations and the beginning evidence and the possible perjuries and then go to indictments.

"I'm not going to try to predict the outcome, Marshall," Web continued. "But I'm going to make the record show that the moment I heard about this I took the proper actions for a Portran director. That's more than I can say for Henry Donaldson. Poor Henry, I think he thinks that if he never does anything to hurt anyone, he'll go to heaven — even when he ignores other people's sinning when he hears about it. I don't think the rules work that way — rules for getting into heaven, I mean. If Henry doesn't look out he'll go to hell, not heaven, and he will be very unhappy there."

The FBI team came to Portran on schedule, having asked the principal executives ahead of time, as is customary, to bring to the meeting their personal income tax returns and any and all data in their files relating to political contributions. Because of a telephone call to the FBI initiated by the attorney representing Marshall Lee, they called him in first and were not surprised when, after answering a few preliminary identification questions, he refused to talk. They were unprepared, however, for the action, to a man, of all the other Portran executives whom they next sought to interrogate. Each marched in, provided copies of all the items requested and then, from Frank Abbott on down, announced he would answer no questions on the grounds that to do so might be incriminating. The FBI team spent an extra day perusing documents, then left.

A few days later, an attorney from the Justice Department telephoned Marshall Lee's attorney. A week following that, Frank Abbott and the other Portran officers were again visited, this time by two Justice Department attorneys. They told Frank Abbott and each of his associates that they had reason to suspect that illegal political donation practices existed at Portran and, in particular, they told Frank Abbott that they had evidence linking him to an Italian money-laundering firm and to illegal cash transfers to Congressman Angus Fields. Again, Frank Abbott and all his staff refused to answer questions.

While Web was waiting to see what the government would do next, he was surprised to receive in the mail his copy, as a Portran Inc. shareholder, of Frank Abbott's letter to all shareholders. This communiqué was surprising and puzzling to Web. Abbott's letter stated first that, in the routine regular visiting of leading American corporations by the FBI to investigate whether illegal political contributions were being made, he and other executives of Portran had recently been included. Abbot then went on to state that Portran's executives, all patriotic citizens, had made individual political contributions. All were entirely personal and legal and did not involve the company. Since it unfortunately has become common to regard anyone who finances political candidates as representing so-called "special interests," Abbott said, such individuals increasingly run the risk of being subjects of witch-hunts by government bureaucrats. He pointed out that records on everything from personal income taxes to contributions of every kind were made available to the FBI. Abbott and the other Portran officers, he reported, had chosen not to cooperate with the government, however, in its attempts to subject them to unnecessary, detailed, lengthy, personal interrogations. Government action here, Abbot's letter stated, was nothing more than fishing, in the hopes of uncovering something in the individual's actions that they could possibly misinterpret as illegal. Abbott closed by saying he was happy to announce that the investigating of Portran by the government apparently had been discontinued, the government presumably having decided that nothing improper existed about any actions taken by Portran's executives.

Then Big Frank's letter had a final peculiarly worded paragraph. Expressing his own belief that the over-investigating of political donations by the government was likely to grow, Abbott announced that a new policy had been established at Portran regarding political donations. Portran and its principal executives would make no political contributions whatsoever in the future. In this way, Portran's managers could ensure they would not suffer further harassment and the concentration of their energies on the management of Portran would not be diluted.

What, Web asked himself, did that announcement mean? It sounded like — could it be? — that Big Frank had had a real scare with the Marshall Lee action. Maybe he was going to end his entire political king-making effort. No more illegal contributions. No more pressure on his executives to co-operate. No more funds siphoned off from Portran in an effort to build the political career of Angus Fields.

Web could not telephone big Frank to ask what it all meant. He had already skipped one Portran board meeting. It took place while the Justice Department attorneys were around, and Web could not bring himself to be in a meeting with Big Frank at that time. The U.S. Attorney General's office may have believed that they could not yet prove Marshall Lee's allegations and so decided to go on hold. If it was over for the time being, should he go to the government himself? Why? He had no evidence. He could only repeat what Marshall Lee told him, of which accusations they were already aware. Web could now resign from the board and let Frank get himself a new friendly director. It would be a relief to sever that relationship.

Neither Web nor Henry had telephoned the other after the meeting in Big Frank's office. Web was still annoyed with Henry's lack of backbone. On the other hand, he knew perfectly well that Henry was unhappy with him for being so quick to accuse Big Frank. Henry had often chided Web for his snobbishness toward Big Frank. Henry had repeatedly told Web he should be more tolerant of Frank's ways.

"You don't like him because of his language and appearance and style as much as anything else," Henry once told Web, an accusation Web had denied although he realized he loathed Big Frank's crudeness. "To you, Big Frank will always be a truck driver even though he is one of the country's most successful entrepreneurs and CEOs. He's just not in your fraternity. If I, with my upbringing, can accept him, Web, why can't you?"

Web knew Henry had a point. But there were other differences between Web and Big Frank. Frank's approach to management was far from Web's — too tough, too ruthless with his own personnel, with competitors, and even with customers. Also, Frank's political biases were too extreme for Web. Web believed Henry felt the same way but was simply more tolerant.

Web thought of telephoning Henry, but he needed a good reason. He could hardly call and pretend the conversation in Frank's office hadn't happened and say something like, "Henry, I wonder whether you know anything I don't know that would explain exactly what Frank Abbott is up to with his announcement to the shareholders. What does the last paragraph about no future political contributions by Portran's executives really mean?"

Then, much to Web's surprise, Henry Donaldson's secretary phoned to say that Mr. Donaldson wanted to come and see Mr. Webster. An hour later, Henry sat down in Web's office and accepted a cup of tea — which he sipped slowly, seemingly enjoying being again in the presence of a good friend. Harold Webster was mystified by the unusual repose on Henry Donaldson's part. Web had expected Henry to be extremely nervous in this first meeting since their falling out, but it was the other way around. Web was the one not completely at ease.

"Web, you've got a nice office here. It's big, but it's warm. I like that mahogany paneling and all those books. It's the world's largest, and most handsome, library of old books about merchandising. It's fitting for you. You're an old merchandiser."

Henry put his cup down and looked at Web with fondness. "Web, are you still mad at me? You know, I was mad at you, too — for, well, I guess all of five minutes. You were mad at me longer than that. And you were entitled to it, I know. But unlike you, I didn't have a chance to stay mad long. Frank Abbott took care of that. I'll bet, Web, you haven't the slightest idea what happened after you left Big Frank's office that day."

Web now was totally confused as to what was going on here — Henry sitting there so calm and, yes, actually enjoying himself.

"Yes, Henry, you're right. I don't have the slightest idea. What did happen? Except, of course, I know that as soon as I left the room, Big Frank got up and, to reward you for your display of absolute confidence in him, gave you a big kiss. So, I'm glad to see you're well again. Your doctor put you on antibiotics, I'm sure."

"No, Web. Frank was appreciative of my accepting his proposal — the one you refused so flatly — that we leave Marshall Lee to him and go tend to our own businesses. But he showed his appreciation in not so physical a way as you have suggested. He was more — what shall I say? — oratorical.

"He started by attributing what he called my loyalty to him not only to confidence in him personally, but as arising also from admiration for his strong personal commitment to influencing the political scene. He then made a speech — and every word he sired will live forever in my memory — about how the liberals and socialists are intent on taking over this nation and destroying free enterprise. And how there are these namby-pambys — like you, Web. He used some adjectives and phrases for you that I never heard before, and didn't catch all of exactly, but I think one meant you play with yourself in public. Then he put it in high gear and began to fume. You, Web, he said, are typical of big businessmen too stupid to realize business is being ruined by a government controlled by the enemies of business. All these unconstitutional laws! He was determined, he emphasized, to go on doing what he was doing. It was his constitutional right. He wasn't afraid of being attacked and if worse came to worst, and his accusers were believed, he would take the issues to the Supreme Court and win. There was nothing wrong — by now he was in his voice's highest range in both volume and bandwidth — with using Portran funds to advance the free enterprise system because that was good for the stockholders — and good for the stockholders was precisely what he was employed to create. He told me that, the same as he had gotten rid of you as a director, he wouldn't have any officer around who would refuse to put in his share. No executive who refused to invest in America deserves as big a year-end bonus as one who does.

"Then," continued Henry, "he began to brag about the smart ways in which he had been beating the system. He told me about the phony consulting firm in Italy. He told me how he fed them the names of various companies he pretended he was considering buying and told them to send him reports — that were really publicly available data they could take off the Internet about each company in a few minutes at no real cost. He held them to a fee of four hundred thousand a year, essentially all clear profit to them, but he had them charge Portran over two million, he said. That money difference went to their New York office and was delivered back to him in cash.

"That Portran money was used to fund Fields. Frank claimed he had Angus Fields absolutely under his control. Fields was going to be a cabinet member, then a senator, Portran's senator, Big Frank's senator, and by God, Fields was going to eventually become a successful candidate for President."

"Wait a minute, Henry," interrupted Web. "You've got to tell me — how were you doing throughout all this disclosure? How was your heartbeat, how was your breathing, when he was telling you this? I know you well, Henry. Here just a few minutes before you had seen me get kicked out and here he was feeling safe in confessing criminal actions to you. Didn't you regard that as a bit insulting?"

"Web — how shall I say this? I had a feeling come over me like nothing I've ever known before. I said, Frank, don't say anything more. You've said enough.

"That startled him — he stopped dead in his tracks. He looked at me, and I've never seen such a look on Big Frank's face — and you know he's got this repertoire of amazingly murderous looks. Well, I just went on. I said I was going to divulge what he told me. I was going to back up Marshall Lee.

"Then I told him that he is going to jail and Portran is going to take a hell of a beating because all its top executives are involved. I said he should forget Angus Fields, because with my repeating what Frank told me, plus Marshall Lee's story, it is not Lee alone against Frank any longer!

"Frank glared at me — I mean fiercely. I would say that if he'd had an axe handy right then he would have split my head in two with one vertical whack."

Henry paused. He rubbed his chin, and then straightened his tie very slowly.

"Do you know what, Web? I suddenly didn't give a damn about Frank's anger at me. You have to understand. It was not just the way he exposed himself — and what that added up to — what that meant to me as a director of the company. It was the way he had assumed I was his boy -- that I would never repeat anything he told me.

"That got to me, Web, and I found myself with the inspiration to make a proposal to him. I reminded him that I was an attorney and I told him that he had a choice. He could stop all these shenanigans — call all his buddies in and tell them the game was over — cancel all of his arrangements with that Italian consulting firm — tell Angus Fields he was not going to see another dime — get himself out of politics — get Portran and all its executives out of it. I would leave it to him to do that. But if he didn't do it, then he had me to contend with. And Web, after I said that, I just walked out of the room."

Both friends then sat quietly, saying nothing, enjoying the shared contemplation, smiling, nodding, and looking at each other restfully.

Then Henry broke the silence with "Web, there's something else I can tell you about, that you probably don't know."

"So tell me, Henry" quickly replied Web, now completely relaxed, confident that what Henry would now add would not be disturbing.

"I called Marshall Lee and asked him a question you didn't ask him, namely, why was he doing this? I told him that here he's been the henchman for Big Frank, running for Frank this illegal political contributions operation, and then suddenly he decides to bring in the FBI. Why? And he right away told me."

"Yes — so? So what did he tell you?"

"He said the FBI had called him out of the blue. That is how all of this began. The FBI said they had an anonymous written tip describing the illegal Portran operation and naming him, Lee, as the one who could best be the source of detail. Lee knew right away it was his wife who sent the memo because she had said she would do exactly that. You know, Lee's got this nasty divorce going on. He had told his wife what he was doing for Big Frank. That was dumb, but that he did. They quarreled about it continually, Lee said. She thought Big Frank should pay Lee a big bribe to keep his mouth shut and was angry Lee didn't push for it. His wife especially hated him, Lee told me, because he hadn't made enough money for her to capture in the divorce.

"So when the FBI came at Lee with that memo, he knew they wouldn't stop until they got the whole story and so he was in the soup for sure now. So he talks to his attorney who of course says he'll get him immunity in a deal if he co-operates with the FBI, and tells all. That's it, Web. No mystery about Lee."

"Portran's executives are all going to get big fines, aren't they, Henry? But Big Frank—he's going to jail, isn't he?"

"Yes, Web. I think Big Frank's going to jail. But it will take a while, wouldn't you guess? His lawyers will appeal and appeal. Meanwhile, we directors will have to get Big Frank to resign and get a new CEO. Neither job will be fun."

"At least the directors won't be in any personal danger — not having known," added Web.

"No danger from the government, no, Web. But the stockholders will sue us when the share price goes to hell. Their attorneys will claim we should have known" countered Henry.

"So there's no early end of this adventure for us directors, is there?" sighed Web.

"No, Web. We're just at the beginning. But, at least, my friend, we'll have each other's company — and we'll survive."

Chapter 10: A Matter of Black and White

Bill White, slouched in his seat with his head back and his eyes closed, was nearing home, a company chauffeur at the wheel. It had been a long, tiring day at the office, they were stuck in traffic, and he was glad he was not doing the driving. His thoughts drifted back to two weeks before when he had been driving home himself and had switched on the car radio to hear the seven o'clock news. He then had been startled by the newscaster's quoting of an unnamed White House source to the effect that Georgia White was a leading candidate for appointment by the President to head the new cabinet level Department of Environmental Preservation. Bill knew a White House staffer had discussed the possibility with his wife, Georgia, a nationally prominent environmental law expert, on the phone a week before. But Georgia had as yet received no further word.

When Bill heard that news item, his first reaction had been pride. The President could not make a better selection for the DEP post, he thought. During the five years he had been president of Eskimo Corporation, he twice had had to deal with a situation where a company executive would not move to suit company needs because his wife's career would have been impaired. Bill had found those incidents annoying and had become prejudiced against promoting men with professional wives to critical company positions — with no thought that he personally might be involved in the same problem one day.

If the cabinet appointment did indeed come about, the Whites had agreed they would lease an apartment in Washington and retain their West Coast home. With Eskimo having gone international, and federal government policy and actions becoming increasingly influential on business decisions, he was already finding himself in Washington often. Because the company had expanded into Europe, he could easily justify being in the East more frequently in the future, and Georgia could often fly west for weekends. Still, there would be very substantial separation and he knew he would hate that.

When he had reached his home that earlier day, he had been surprised by media reporters surrounding his automobile. He had had difficulty getting away from them and up to his house. Slamming the entry door behind him, he had grabbed the nearest phone to try to get hold of Richard Cantor. As he did so, Georgia had appeared from the study and he recalled now how relieved he had felt then to discover that she happened to have arrived home before the news peoples' assault and had wisely directed the housekeeper to say Mrs. White was not available.

Georgia immediately had informed Bill that Cantor had telephoned as soon as he, like the reporters, had heard that news report, and already was on his way to their home. When Cantor drove up, he staved off the news people with promises he would call them later to say when Georgia might be ready to talk to the press. Cantor had immediately expressed the hunch that the reporters must have picked up some more concrete facts than those in the news report. That might mean Georgia was definitely chosen and would soon hear from the President.

During the two weeks that followed, the papers produced background pieces, speculations, and anecdotes. Georgia, still merely only rumored to be the nominee for the new member of the President's cabinet, was always described as an exceptionally successful attorney specializing in environmental issues.

Eskimo's other executives and their spouses had long been accustomed to Georgia's being prominent on her own. Few corporation presidents' wives also happen to be senior partners of leading law firms. The other company wives always had been jealous of Georgia and they all now resented having to adjust to a heightened sense of relative inferiority. But her new status as a possible cabinet member also had its favorable repercussions within the company family. Alfred Albritton, the chairman of the board, was enthusiastic. He had been a co-founder decades ago of the frozen food company that became today's giant Eskimo Corporation.

"This will be terrific for the company, Bill," he had exclaimed. "If Georgia goes to Washington, I'll make you Eskimo's board chairman. It's time for me to retire anyway. We'll promote Marc Stanley to president and have him run the day-to-day operations. You'll spend most of your time in the East pushing our expansion into Europe and pulling off more acquisitions. Many people will now be more aware of Eskimo because of Georgia. With Georgia in the President's cabinet, you'll get to people who will lead you to deals you never could arrange otherwise. You'll mix with influential leaders from every country on the globe. The company will double as we go international. This is a marvelous opportunity. And by the way — Georgia will make a hell of a cabinet member."

So it had appeared there would be no trouble in Eskimo from Georgia's possible appointment. The obstacle, if any, would be the "hazard," as they had always referred to a certain incident of their past. During the two weeks that had elapsed since that first news report out of Washington,

Georgia and Bill had oscillated between deep anxiety about the hazard and confidence that they need not be concerned at all over it. Bill had argued that it was unlikely reporters would come upon information they had no reason to search for, some from before he was born. She had chided him for wishful thinking and reminded him that what was really of greatest danger occurred only twenty-five years before, not fifty.

"Well, that's not likely to be exposed either," he had assured her. "And if it were to come out — sometime after you joined the cabinet — it certainly would not constitute any reason for your having to resign."

"Maybe not. Let's just realize that we'll be gambling on the hazard's staying hidden," she had responded.

This review by Bill of the previous two weeks halted as seven o'clock approached and Bill asked the driver to turn on the radio. The very first news item jolted him. A nurse in Cottonville, South Carolina, the report said, claimed Georgia to be the young woman who twenty-five years earlier had given birth to a little girl at a hospital there. The seventy-six year old nurse, Sarah Lee Jones, was heard on the interviewer's tape saying: "It was easy to remember Georgia Washington, when I saw her face in the newspaper yesterday. I knew right away she was the girl I took care of. She was a real beauty, that one, and such a sweet girl. And that name! I couldn't forget that. I remember she told me that every first-born boy in her family — for generations — was always named George, and the girls, Georgia. Can you just imagine? And besides, the baby was black!"

So, thought Bill, his heart racing, the "hazard" has made its public debut! Saying nothing to the driver, he got out as soon as the car stopped, with no surprise at again finding reporters in his way and hurrying through them to his front door. This time Dick Cantor was already on hand because this story had broken before the seven o'clock news. Georgia, fortunately, had again arrived home earlier. Cantor was on the telephone. He hung up and turned to them. They all stared at each other for a moment, each wondering where to start.

Then Cantor said: "I've just been talking to Cottonville — the hospital there in South Carolina. Of course, it's after ten o'clock back East. But I got a lady in the office to check the files. She could find no record of a patient in that hospital in the 40s named Georgia Washington. This Sarah Lee Jones sounds like a publicity seeker — or she has some screws loose. Georgia, were you ever in South Carolina delivering a little black kid? A lot more nuts will turn up because of all the publicity you have received. Why don't we nip this in the bud by my issuing a denial to the press? I don't think you're required to comment about each and every claim some nut makes. So let me take care of it."

Georgia looked at Dick Cantor and at Bill, then said:

"Let's all sit down. Sarah Lee Jones remembered my maiden name, Washington, which I must have mentioned to her, but I was registered in the hospital under my married name, Mrs. William White. There was a special reason why I went to Cottonville — where Bill's mother lived — to have that baby. But perhaps Bill had better tell you about that."

Cantor looked stunned, then quickly recovered his composure.

"But all the bios I have on you, Bill, and the material that has appeared in the newspapers, say your parents were from Greenfield, South Carolina. I have them coming out here before you were born. Where did Cottonville get into the act?"

"Cottonville's a little suburb of Greenfield, Dick. My parents came west just as your biographical information has it. But their life in California isn't important. I think we have to talk about South Carolina."

Bill paused a moment, looked at Georgia, then went on.

"My mother, Dorothy, was born and raised in Cottonville. Her mother — my grandmother — I never knew her — but I was told she could have passed as a white. She had my mother by my white grandfather and my mother definitely could — and did — pass. When my mother was sixteen, she went to work as a live-in household helper in Greenfield. Girls from Cottonville did that. It was a short bus ride away.

"The household Dorothy went to was my father's. He was a bachelor who lived with his elderly aunt. He ran the family business, which he inherited — a general store, a small department store, I guess you would call it. He was Adolph Schwartz then, not Allen White. The Schwartzes came from Germany in the early 1800s. They were in their fifth generation in South Carolina. He gave my mother a job clerking in the store where the customers took her for white. He was her teacher — she was twenty years younger — and he fell in love with her. She was a very pretty lady — loving, bright, generous, kind. I know she worshipped my father and he her. When his aunt died, he sold the store and came west with my mother — she was then nineteen. They were married out here — and he changed his name from Schwartz — "black" in German — to White. He had a sense of humor.

"They worried about the color problem. When I was getting ready to be born, so my mother told me, they had no idea how they would handle the situation if I had emerged with an embarrassingly dark skin. But I didn't, and I was kept ignorant of my black ancestry until after my father's death."

"Let's see, Bill, you were in the marines when your father died, weren't you?"

"Yes, Dick. I joined up when I finished high school, and I was discharged in a couple of years, because my back was slightly injured in a helicopter accident. When my father died, my mother went back to Cottonville. I visited her on my first leave. You can imagine what an event that visit was for me, because it was then that I learned about my mother's background. I learned she had always been lonely out here. She wanted to return to her "own country," as she expressed it, and she did just that after dad passed away. She was well off, of course. Dad invested his store money brilliantly in the right California real estate and made a pile out here, as you know. His estate went into a trust fund, with my mother and me sharing the income until her death. Then it all came to me.

"She had a large house in Cottonville on the edge of the white district where it bordered on the black area. St. Simon's University, the large black medical and dental school, is in Cottonville. My mother boarded black girl college students and supported their education. She made me agree to lead a separate white life. She was confident that if I did not visit her then she could keep her black ancestry out of my white society thousands of miles away. Well, it's worked that way — up until today."

"Listen, both of you," interrupted Cantor. "You don't have to go into any more of this with me than you feel like. Let me get at the crucial question though — even if there is more we'll have to talk about. Maybe I'm off here — but I take it you found a way to divest yourself of that whole situation."

"Denials won't work if that's what you're thinking," Bill blurted out. "My mother was well known in Cottonville. It's a small town with a university attached. A few old people are still around — in addition to that nurse — who might remember and speak to reporters about something that will connect. And the hospital and the county will have some kind of records of the baby's birth."

Bill stopped to take a deep breath, then went on.

"Georgia and I decided we wanted to be man and wife — despite my background. We decided that we might adopt children but would have none of our own. We would take no chances."

"It was a plan not fully thought out," added Georgia, "I was career-minded, and having children didn't interest me — then."

"It wasn't just my having to take on the sudden handicap of being a black, if we had a black child," said Bill. "It would be going against the decision my parents made for me for the whole pattern of my life. Hell, I was white by any way I cared to judge. Two whites with a black child? Can you imagine my dragging Georgia into such a situation? I don't have to go on about that. But — Georgia and I … well, there was an accident."

"Dick, we were scared to death," said Georgia. "Two months before our scheduled June wedding, I discovered I was pregnant and I didn't want an abortion. I was sure our child would be white. After our wedding, we kept talking about it, and Bill was determined that we should play it cautiously.

"So, with our friends thinking I was in my sixth month while actually I was approaching the eighth, we went to Cottonville for the Christmas holidays. We told everyone it was to spend them with Bill's mother — but, of course — well — she came to the hotel to visit with us. Her friends didn't know we were there. It was very cloak and dagger.

"Our plan was that if the baby were born black, unlikely as we thought that would be, then Bill's mother would take it and would get it adopted by black parents. Our friends would be told I had a miscarriage while away. When the baby was delivered — and it was black — all preplanning was of no interest to me at first. I was confused and frightened, of course, but I wanted to keep my baby. It was a little girl. But Bill was adamant, and he acted quickly — and I gave in. It was easy for Bill to arrange things secretly through his mother."

No one talked for a moment. Georgia looked at Bill sadly, arose, gave him a light kiss on the forehead, thinking how much she loved this sweet, handsome man, then sat down on the arm of his chair. Despite their discussions during the preceding days, they did not have a ready plan as to exactly what to do if they found they had guessed wrong and the story about their child came out — except that they would not deny it and would face it squarely.

Bill and Georgia were not uncomfortable in bringing out the story to Dick Cantor. He was a long-time close friend and an Eskimo officer. It was Dick who had persuaded Al Albritton to offer the presidency of Eskimo to Bill, pulling Bill away from the law firm in which Georgia was still a partner. Georgia had had involvement in state party politics and was nationally prominent in environmental law. But that background did not make her expert in handling problems like this one. Bill's habit was to depend on Dick, Eskimo's vice president for communications, on all public relations issues. That added up to an automatic assignment for Dick Cantor.

"Let me get something straight," said Dick. "You don't want to try to keep this thing as quiet as possible. You're saying that the facts have to come out all the way?"

"Two weeks ago — when all this publicity on Georgia's possible cabinet appointment started — we were slightly concerned that this past circumstance might be exposed,"

Bill replied. "Now I'm certain nothing in our backgrounds is going to be left unexplored. We made only careful contact with my mother after leaving the baby with her — just phone calls. She was immovable on this for fear of creating problems for us somehow.

"We learned of her death because the bank out here acted on the trust fund when her local lawyer called to inform the bank. No one in her small circle of friends or relatives back there ever sought to contact us, which means that they didn't know about the connection. Or, if anyone did -- that lawyer for example, whom my mother obviously told of the trust but maybe nothing else -- they were all pledged to secrecy. I know my mother's earlier lawyer, the one she used when the baby was born, has been dead for years."

Dick Cantor, as the senior public relations executive of a large corporation, approached most problems that arose with two rules. One was that you bragged publicly when you had something to brag about. You did it in a dignified and carefully thought-out way so as to get the maximum benefit. The other was that if you were up against damaging information you tried to minimize it without violating the law or being unethical. You tried to put the best possible face on it.

What the Whites now were confronted with was not exactly in his field and he knew that. His first concern was about Bill's image with company employees and executives, big customers, members of the board of directors, stockholders, and merger prospect company's CEOs. He knew there was no way to totally insulate the company from Bill and Georgia's situation. The events of decades ago added up to a set of conflicting issues and there was no certainty about the outside reactions. They had abandoned their baby, and Bill had essentially cut his mother out of his life — as though neither had ever existed. How would their friends and associates feel about that? What about the reaction of the President's advisors, the public at large? He did not want to jump to any conclusions.

"Let me go home and think about this — and sleep on it. I'll tell the media right away that you both are unavailable for comment but that I'll get back to them tomorrow. By not issuing an immediate denial to this report from Cottonville, however, that's the same as telling the reporters that there is something to it. By tomorrow, reporters and investigators will be down in Cottonville — and Greenfield — some of whom probably will be working for the White House or the Senate confirmation committee. You're right, Bill. Your whole life's story, accurate or not, will be in the papers and on the radio and TV news.

"There's one thing you'd better tell me more about though, before I get away. What about the child? Where is she? Who is she? What did your mother do with her?"

"We don't know," replied Bill. "The hospital and the doctor signed some papers regarding the birth, and we both signed a formal release to turn the baby over for adoption legally to my mother. She said that she knew how and would take care of shifting the child to others — that no records of the transfer would end up with our names on them. That's all we have any knowledge of."

"What do you mean, no names on records?"

"Dick, my mother had this big house in Cottonville. She had lots of girls living there, mostly students at the college. But she also took care of girls who were with child out of wedlock. In those years, it was easy to move newborn black babies about in that county — other parents taking an additional child — a childless couple wanting a baby. The new parents doubtless simply had the child recorded as born as their own. All you needed to get a fresh birth certificate was an affidavit, which could even be written well after the birth. Birth certificates most likely were issued late most of the time then — what with midwives and amateur midwives often doing some black births, not doctors — and those births often in homes, not in hospitals. Money placed with the new parents would guarantee fast action. Suffice it to say that if my mother wanted to cover it up she could. She did, I'm sure. The only way the reporters could find the child would be if the adopting parents had been told — by my mother — who the real parents were — and she never would have done that."

Back in his apartment Dick Cantor left his bed-table radio turned to the news station and stepped back out to the living room to see if the last piece of the eleven p.m. TV news might have something more about the Whites. But they were off on sports and the weather and Dick turned off the TV and got into bed.

Dick was deep in sleep when the telephone rang and he sought out the bed lamp's switch with difficulty. It was after midnight and Dick wondered who could be calling at that hour. He thought it might be Georgia or Bill with some important new development. It was Alfred Albritton instead. "I should have guessed," said Dick to himself. Alfred knew Dick Cantor well enough to know he would be sound asleep at midnight, but Alfred didn't care what time he called Dick if he wanted to talk.

"Dick, I guess you've heard the report on Bill and Georgia's black baby. Now, I've got no prejudice in me, you know that, Dick. But this is serious. I've been sitting here all evening thinking it all out, and I know now that Bill will have to go. Now, there's something that I want you to do, that you're right for, and that's…"

"Al, you're out of your mind!" Dick was now wide-awake and greatly annoyed. He and Alfred Albritton had grown up together and now were growing old together. Dick Cantor's father had been the initial main financial backer of Eskimo and, upon the death of the father, Cantor became a member of the board as well as vice president for communications. Through inheritance, he was the largest stockholder in the company after Albritton. Alfred and Dick were accustomed to talking to each other with frankness, like brothers. Dick's anger made him sarcastic.

"Eskimo is a fair-employment contractor! Do you hear me, Al? You can't discriminate! You're supposed to be putting more blacks on at the executive level!"

"Wait a minute, genius," cut in Al. "You're smart, Dick, but not when you're mad. I didn't call Bill a black. You did. And I'm not saying he has to go next week."

"I don't care if it's next week or next month. You make this decision to fire Bill, you get the Board into it, and it will all be traced right back to the news announcement that has gotten us into this conversation. You haven't suddenly discovered that Bill is incompetent. You'll get a hell of a beating from the government's anti-discrimination people and Bill could file and win a multimillion-dollar damage suit against you. I'll even try to persuade him to sue. And others will be on his side. You'll come out an absolute ass! What a crowning achievement to end your career on! If you think Bill's image is in trouble, what do you think will happen to yours when the media and the government and the community get through with you?"

"Are you serious, Dick? Sometimes I can't tell with you."

"You'd damned well better believe I'm serious, Al! Have you told any of the Board members that you plan to push Bill out?"

"No, you're the first person I called. But what the hell — I decide these things. The Board goes along. You know that."

"Not on this they won't just go along. They're not dumb, Al. They'll see the issues. They won't want to get into a mess to please you. They don't need that. For that matter, they don't need Eskimo board membership — most of us don't, at least. Besides, Bill has a position with them. He's been a good president and they know it. They'll give you big trouble. Now, what was the damn-fool task you were going to assign to me?"

"I wanted you to talk to Bill first, tomorrow morning, ahead of me."

"And tell him what — that you are a man with no racial prejudice?"

"That his success — as president of Eskimo — has been in great part because of his skill as a negotiator in contracts and mergers — and in presentations to customers, and to stock market analysts, and to the shareholders, and the government — and that he was able to represent the company so well because everybody trusted him. He has been the tower of integrity. He has never misrepresented anything even a tiny bit. But now he has misrepresented himself. When anyone deals with him, they'll wonder what else he's covering up. That's a beginning, but I'll leave it at that. Notice that I didn't mention his Negro blood. That's not really the issue. Look, Dick — it's not like an executive who maybe has a thing going with a secretary and gets into a messy divorce. This is a different caliber of problem. It's more like fraud. But I will say this in general: If a man mishandles his personal life enough so that people lose confidence in him — he can't be president of Eskimo."

"God Almighty, Al! You amaze me! You're so far from an intelligent discussion of this problem — let alone having a compassionate, humane, fair approach to it — although I don't know I'm surprised. But I do agree that Georgia and Bill's situation requires that you ask yourself, in an un-frenzied, calm way, if anything has changed — in view of the disclosure of, and the public's interest in, the private life and the background of the company's president? Now, I have a suggestion regarding that question."

"O.K., what is it? I'm listening. Maybe not very intelligently by your standards but with all the brainpower I can muster in my old head."

"It's this: you ought to ask me to take on a study of the matter by probing it with all the outside board members — then putting the conclusions together into a recommendation for you, as chairman, for board action — if any."

"Would the probing include probing with the board the question of Bill's resigning?"

"It would be an objective study. If that specific question should be raised, it would get worked over" replied Dick.

"What do you mean, if? I've already raised it."

"This study wouldn't be concerned with what you think. It would be done for you as board chairman — by me, a director — to let you know what the board members are thinking — and why."

"Why don't I just go and ask them what they think? Why do I need you? It's my board. I picked them. They should just tell me directly what they recommend."

"It isn't your company," replied Dick firmly and very slowly for intended emphasis. "It's a public company even though you hold a big block of the shares. The directors are not yours. They represent the stockholders. Let's quit this talk — you know all this. You called me, not the directors. You know you can't go and ask them anything — with your knack for answering while asking. To protect yourself, you have to have an objective study."

"O.K. I'll stay out of it. You go interrogate the board. But I know how it'll turn out. There's only one answer to come up with. You'll produce it. You'll recommend that Bill go — for all the good, sound reasons. When will you be able to talk to the other directors?"

"Soon — that is, if you'll let me go back to sleep."

"Let's split up the problems," Dick said the next morning at the White's home. "First, there is Georgia and the President's cabinet. We should seek to preserve the truth, Georgia — that you are superb for the job. Whether the President ends up sticking with you or not, we still want the majority of Americans and all of your friends, associates, clients — everyone that counts — to believe that you're qualified in every way.

"The second problem concerns <u>your</u> image, Bill. Last week, if you had announced yourself as available, you would have been given serious consideration by ten big corporations who might have top executive openings looming. Today, you would not get on their lists at all. We need to fight that."

He stopped a moment to see if Bill or Georgia wanted to comment, then continued.

"The third problem is your relations, Bill, with the company, Eskimo."

He related his phone conversation with Al Albritton the preceding night. Bill wasn't surprised by Dick's report, but his face disclosed that emotional pressure was being tightly contained. Dick sensed Bill's anger and Georgia watched Bill with concern. Dick knew it was striking them for the first time that no matter how brilliantly they now strategized, their future would not possess the firm base of absolute respect and admiration that always had been shown them by everyone they had ever dealt with, socially or professionally.

In telling them of Albritton's phone call, Dick had not violated a confidence. He knew Albritton expected him to pass along those remarks. This was Albritton's way of using Dick to soften Bill up, planting the seed for Bill to resign. So Dick pointed this out to Bill.

"If quitting comes to your mind, Bill, throw it out as unworthy. We're going to lick Al with his own crony board. Don't look at me like that! We will! You'll see! But we have to get to Georgia's statement.

"The 6:00 p.m. news in the East sets our timing," continued Dick. "The media will stand still if they get something good enough by 5:00 p.m. in the East — that's 2:00 p.m. here. We can make it, of course. I tried something for a starter early this morning. Let me read this out loud."

Dick then read his draft. The draft started out with Georgia and Bill having fallen in love in college. It told of Bill's partial black ancestry and the fact that Georgia knew of it before marrying him. It emphasized that she had no regrets in her marriage, that both felt fortunate in being husband and wife to each other. As to the baby, the statement told of their giving it up for adoption. It stressed Georgia's wanting to keep the child and having been willing to face the problem society would present to them. But it went on to say that her husband had prevailed, he having been determined not to subject his wife and child to the prejudice that he believed would have been imposed on his little family.

Then came a difficult, but key, paragraph. It stated that if they had it to do over, if they had possessed then their now fully developed sense of human relations and the set of values they now hold as mature adults, they would not have given their child to others. She stated clearly that they made a mistake when they were very young and were suddenly faced with a problem for which they were not prepared. They both had had to live with the pain and regrets resulting from that decision of decades ago, feelings that would be with them for the rest of their lives because there was no way of rectifying the error.

She and her husband asked for understanding and forgiveness of the actions they had taken long ago.

"Dick," said Georgia when he had finished. "That's a great statement. Give me a few minutes to edit slightly and then you can go ahead and release it."

For the next two days, Georgia and Bill White were all over the TV and the papers. While the White House issued no word of any kind, a national debate developed as to whether she should be offered a Cabinet position. Three opinions surfaced. One said that either she was right for the Cabinet or she was not and the appointment should be judged by her competence, not on her having married a part black or her having given up her child for adoption when she was young.

A second opinion argued that she and her husband had been disclosed to be of defective character — racists. The President should not put "that kind of person" in a high government position.

A third view emerged with enthusiastic praise for Georgia. She was guilty of no sin. Her willingness to marry the man she loved although she knew him to be part black, her desire to keep her black child, even her acceding to her husband's wishes and giving up their baby — all were to her credit.

As the days grew to a week, then to two, the issue remained unsettled.

Bill and Georgia meanwhile had avoided a company top-executive party and several other scheduled social events which they had been planning to attend. Bill stayed away from the prestigious Westwood Valley Country Club, not even dropping in for lunch, which he was in the habit of doing two or three times a week. They played no golf and they did not go to the opening of the symphony season. Bill cancelled out on a small luncheon with the visiting Assistant Secretary of the Treasury. He stuck to his office, conferring with the other company executives to a minimum and strictly only about the business at hand. He adopted this pattern because he sensed the embarrassment of others in his presence and wanted to minimize it.

He knew that the problem at Eskimo could not be ignored any longer when Al Albritton poked his head in Bill's office doorway, with an unfamiliar look. He asked if Bill had a few minutes.

First he told Bill how long he had known and admired him. "Bill," he then said, "We've got a problem in the company — in view of this new situation — and I think we ought to face it squarely. I've talked with Dick Cantor a little about it. Maybe he's already talked with you. None of the company executives holds anything against you, least of all me — but a lot of company people and wives are disturbed — well, they're puzzled. I'm not suggesting that what you did makes you out as sort of someone who has falsified himself — but that's what a lot of people are saying — people that you have to deal with in the company and outside the company. You've always had the image of the highest of integrity. You've made lots of deals. You've handled labor problems and mergers. You've always faced the stockholders and customers and security analysts with an image of a straight-talking man who always speaks the truth. We have never tried to cover up problems in the company.

"But your image, Bill, has been sullied — and you know I'm not saying that because it turns out you've got a little colored blood. Hell, we're all part this and that and we've been looking to have more minority people in high places in our company anyway. But, Bill — you're the company president — and even though it was your parents that started it, you're seen now by some as having misrepresented yourself."

"So you're telling me, Al, that you'd like me to resign for the good of the company?" asked Bill, whose facial expression he had kept totally impassive throughout Al's awkward dissertation.

"No, no, Bill! I'm not saying that. I really don't know yet what's best for the company. I just think you and I ought to recognize that we've got a problem, that things aren't the same as they were. And I think you and I ought to ponder what that means. Not jump to any conclusions. Not take precipitous action. Just let's think about it, talk about it. Let's work on it."

"All right," said Bill, rising abruptly. This startled Al Albritton who then also stood up.

"I will ponder it, Al, and I'll tell you what my thoughts are as soon as I've done the necessary deliberating. It won't be long. Thank you for being so frank."

"Look, Bill, I don't want you to think —" started Al as he moved toward the door.

"Don't worry, Al. You did the right thing, coming in and talking to me. You'll hear from me soon," said Bill.

Bill took a telephone call that came in just after Albritton left the office. It was from the head of an executive search firm in the East whom Bill had used for a number of years and who called him for recommendations quite often. It turned out the call was to seek Bill's evaluation of a man Bill knew well who was being considered for a top business position.

When that topic was concluded, Bill said, "Maybe, while you're looking for executives to fill openings — you ought to consider whether there's a need for Bill White to run some promising corporation with headquarters not too far from the nation's capitol. I might have to spend a lot of time on the East Coast in the future, if I want to be near my wife."

He was immediately annoyed with himself for tossing that remark in before hanging up without having planned to. It surely was, he sensed, an emotional reaction to Albrittons' painful recital, but Bill did not know he was capable of reacting stupidly that way.

Meanwhile, a highly influential southern senator, in fact, the chairman of the Senate committee that would ponder the coming cabinet selection and have to approve or reject it, was on the phone with the President's chief of staff. He was saying that it would be very wise for the President to appoint Georgia White to his cabinet.

"I have every reason to believe that she is a very fine lady. My contacts tell me that as to competence in the environment field she is above the other candidates being considered. I think it would be good for the nation — and good for the President — if he were to act immediately — that is, unless you know something I don't know."

The President's assistant thanked the senator and said he would make the senator's views known to the President right away.

The next day a White House aide called Georgia White and asked her to remain near her telephone. Twenty minutes later the President of the United States was on the line. He told her he was certain she would make a distinguished member of his cabinet. He also was confident, he said, that, if she would accept, the Senate would confirm her quickly and the appointment would be of outstanding value to the country. Georgia told him she would be very pleased to have him name her. The official announcement of the nomination was made that afternoon.

Two weeks later Bill and Georgia headed east, Bill to spend a day in some meetings in Baltimore and Georgia to be with the White House staff to prepare for Senate hearings scheduled for the following day. On the evening between, Bill reached Dick Cantor on the phone.

"Dick, you can call off your objective study of how the board members feel about my remaining as president of Eskimo."

"Oh, hell, Bill — I haven't started that survey — I've been stalling. What's up?"

"You can relax, Dick," and Bill told him why.

For a period of less than one hour, the Senate committee questioned Georgia courteously, heard a few minutes each from a small parade of favorable witnesses, and voted unanimously to recommend her confirmation to the full Senate. The Senate's approval came almost immediately. The Whites flew home and Al Albritton came to Bill's office early the next day.

"Bill, I want you and Georgia to know that I congratulate each of you. Georgia's quick confirmation by the Senate was the proper thing. I'm glad the White House had the good sense to name her. And, Bill — I don't know how to say this — but I was wrong when I described a problem for you and me and the company. I overreacted — or I — well, hell, I was just plain wrong. I hope you will forget that conversation. I think all of the other fellows feel the same way — I mean, they want you here. They are more appreciative than ever of what you will be able to do for the company."

"Al, I know about the other executives," replied Bill. "They've all come and spoken to me. But, Al, I'm leaving Eskimo. I've made other plans. I know you'll understand. There is a very strong organization here, so Eskimo doubtless will go on being the number one frozen food supplier in the nation without me."

As Bill drove home that evening, he said to himself that he might have been a bit too generous in his prediction about Eskimo's assured future in his last comment to Al Albritton. After all, the reason Baltimore Canneries wanted him as their new chief executive and made him so generous an offer was because they believed he would build them up by merger and internal development. Bill was confident that Baltimore Canneries, soon to be renamed Baltimore Foods, could become highly successful in frozen foods, a huge market that was certainly growing fast enough to accommodate the entry of an additional supplier.